Praise for *Marry a Mensch*

Devorah offers a rare gift to her readers: a how-to guide to finding your soulmate that is frank, compassionate, and hopeful. With authenticity and humor, she shares the wisdom she has acquired throughout her life's work with singles who are dating for marriage, layered on top of the lessons learned from her own dating journey.

Aleeza Ben Shalom, star of the *Netflix* hit *Jewish Matchmaking*

Marry a Mensch is a masterclass on efficient, confident, and dignified dating. Devorah provides a detailed roadmap that is psychologically sound, rooted in Torah values, and guided by her own journey of self-discovery and spiritual growth. I highly recommend this comprehensive, compassionate, and enlightening book.

Dr. David Lieberman, PhD,
New York Times best-selling author

Devorah Kigel shares practical priceless pearls of dating wisdom that will surely turn into diamonds. Follow her advice and invite us all to the wedding!

Lori Palatnik, author, founding director of Momentum

Devorah is amazing! She was one of the first people I trained in dating mentoring – now there are close to three hundred marriages that she helped create, thank G-d! It's such *nachas* for me – and the world really needs it!

Rosie Einhorn, LCSW

Marry a Mensch is a must-read for anyone navigating the dating process. Devorah's writing style _ _ _ _ funny, deeply insightful, and she cuts right to the heart of the _ _ _ _ _ _ to a savvy friend or mentor who _ _ _ _ ectured at.

T0182530

She will help you gain an understanding of what you actually need in a partner, moving beyond superficial wants that can distract you from what really matters. You will also gain a deeper understanding of yourself and the life you want, to keep you focused and help you actually get there. Dating for marriage can be overwhelming at times, but Devorah walks you through it from soup to nuts, providing invaluable insight to help you navigate the journey.

Sabrina Bendory, author and relationship coach

Having Devorah come along on your dating journey is such a gift. She has an innate ability to break down tough dating dilemmas into simple solutions so you can get to your husband way more quickly. This book provides the comfort of a best friend while at the same time knowing you have a mentor with years of experience on your side. There's no shame involved when working with Devorah's teachings – only wisdom to be gained and lasting love ahead!

Alex Abel Segal, former editor at *Seventeen* magazine

Devorah Kigel, dating coach par excellence, has written a clear and concise dating guide for today's single woman. This book is filled with practical tips and important insights gleaned from her own dating journey as well as her years of successfully guiding hundreds of other women to their soulmates. And…it's a fun read!

Chana Levitan, author and relationship coach

Devorah Kigel has written a terrific, down-to-earth book on dating – a good, fun read, yet packed with incredibly valuable information that will put women on a more painless and rewarding path to Mr. Right.

Gila Manolson, author

Decades of wisdom are packed into this profound yet easy-to-read classic. *Marry a Mensch* is so much more than a dating book – this is a guidebook to living in touch with your inner self and along the way learning how to share that with someone else.

Moshe Gersht, author and TEDx lecturer

Marry a Mensch
Timeless Jewish Wisdom
for Today's Single Woman

Devorah Kigel

gefen
publishing house
JERUSALEM • NEW YORK

Scripture quotations are modified from *The Holy Scriptures According to the
Masoretic Text*, published by the Jewish Publication Society in 1917.

Editor: Kezia Raffel Pride
Cover design: Dragan Bilic
Typesetting: Optume Technologies

ISBN: 978-965-7801-67-3

1 3 5 7 9 8 6 4 2

Gefen Publishing House Ltd.
6 Hatzvi Street
Jerusalem 9438614,
Israel
972-2-538-0247
orders@gefenpublishing.com

Gefen Books
c/o Baker & Taylor Publisher Services
30 Amberwood Parkway
Ashland, Ohio 44805
516-593-1234
orders@gefenpublishing.com

www.gefenpublishing.com.

To arrange speaking engagements for large events or private groups, go to
www.devorahkigel.com

Printed in Israel
Library of Congress Control Number: 2024942245

To my husband Reuven – the mensch I was searching for.
Thank you for always focusing on the best in me.

Contents

Preface

Hi, I'm Devorah Kigel. You must be an amazing woman who is looking to get married. Maybe you've been through a lot of pain and feel that there must be a better way to do this. Or maybe you're just looking for some tips and tricks to make this process a bit easier. Either way, you picked up the right book!

To call my journey to meet my husband a train wreck would be an understatement. Whatever you're experiencing, I've most likely been there, done that. I know the struggle.

I decided to become a dating coach in 2012 to help other women avoid the mistakes I made. And that's also why I wrote this book – to help you navigate your dating journey in a smarter, easier way and hopefully find your husband with clarity and calm. Transforming my pain into my purpose and passion – helping others avoid my mistakes – has been really gratifying and has brought meaning to my challenging journey.

The techniques and mindset shifts that I'm going to share are based on timeless Jewish wisdom and have helped hundreds of my clients marry the right person. This information can help you, too.

Before we begin, let me tell you a bit about my own journey to find the right one.

I grew up completely secular in a very non-Jewish area of Pennsylvania. I went to public school my whole life and then on to secular college after that. This, of course, meant that I was part of the secular singles scene – and it's not pretty.

I always knew that I wanted to get married, and yet I found that the environment I was in, in college and then the New York City singles scene, only made marriage feel impossibly far

Handy Hebrew Helper: A *shidduch* is a match made by a matchmaker, who may be either a professional or simply a friend, mentor, or family member who has an idea for a suitable mate.

away. There was such a lack of respect for women, and the guys I was meeting were so disingenuous and so focused on the wrong things. I started to despair of ever finding someone decent.

I spent two years in Paris getting my master's degree and decided to see if the French dating scene was any different. Can you guess what I discovered? It's not that different…

After leaving France, I came to New York City, where I met Orthodox Jews for the first time in my life and was introduced to the Jewish way of dating.

Wait – there's *a Jewish way of dating*?

Actually, yes!

I discovered, for instance, that instead of dating for fun and realizing six months (or six years) later that you're incompatible, Orthodox Jews first determine compatibility and only afterwards start investing emotionally. I learned that taking the physical off the table enables you to evaluate a date without your brain being clouded. I remember this hitting me like a ton of bricks – this way of dating is genius!

How many heartbreaks this would have saved me… I wanted in.

It happened gradually, with a lot of challenges along the way, but eventually, I adopted the Jewish way of dating. I actually realized that since Judaism had so much wisdom regarding dating and relationships, perhaps it had wisdom in other areas as well (which led me to becoming more observant).

However, my dating journey was not over. I spent a year learning in seminary (a school for religious studies) in Israel to beef up my Jewish education and observance. During that time, I was set up on a *shidduch* date. Nice guy, but not for me.

Unfortunately, I was so jaded, cynical, and discouraged by this point in my dating journey that I was ready to settle for someone I was incompatible with. I had basically given up. People kept telling me I would never find what I was looking for, and I felt betrayed by my heart. It had led me astray so many times. Maybe I really did need to make a decision with *only* my head? Here was a nice guy. He would make a good father. I figured that was enough. We got engaged.

We spent a month arguing, and I didn't even want to admit how stifled I felt. I wish I had had a dating coach to tell me about sticking to your deal-breaker list! I was so convinced that I would never get married otherwise that I committed to go through with it.

Then, I went to my friend's engagement party, where I saw one of my rabbis. He took one look at me and knew that something wasn't right. "Devorah, how's engagement?" he said.

"You know, engagement is hard," I replied. (Which it is, but not *this* hard!)

He looked at me and said, "You know, breaking off an engagement is easier than getting divorced." Mic drop.

Wait, what? Did he just say BREAK my engagement? *I can't do that*, I thought. *I already told everyone I'm getting married!* I was so horrified at the thought of how humiliating it would be to break it off that I was willing to go through with the wedding just to avoid being embarrassed!

But slowly, the realization that I might be marrying the wrong person sank in. And I realized that was a *much more horrifying* possibility. Thank God, I got up the courage to break it off. I left Israel in a tumult of drama and heartbreak. I remember thinking, *Ok, that's it – I'll be a cat lady – I'm never getting married*. I was on the brink of despair.

And then, three months later, my husband picked me up in synagogue on the Upper West Side of Manhattan. I had found my mensch. That was over twenty-five years ago! Turns out, you

Handy Hebrew Helper: *Middos* means "measures." It's the Hebrew word that is used to describe a person's character traits – kind, caring, curious, responsible, ambitious, etc. A person's *middos* are very hard to change, which is why we want to focus more on these qualities than on anything external.

don't have to choose between *middos* and muscles! You *can* be attracted to a nice guy!

So, ladies, I've been there. I've made all the mistakes. I've allowed my heart to lead me blindly and been totally let down! But I've also tried to ignore my feelings and just follow my head, and that didn't work either. That's why I tell my clients that you have to *lead with your head* and bring your heart and hormones along *after*! As it turns out, this is the perfect middle ground – the best way to find a guy you love who also makes sense for you.

What I'm going to share with you in this book is geared to everyone, regardless of where you stand on the religious spectrum. My clients include women from all walks of life, all ages, first and second marriages, Sephardi and Ashkenazi, religiously observant and totally secular. So don't worry – whoever you are, this book is for you.

Now, let's begin. I'm going to hold your hand and guide you through the process with humor and hope.

If you have any questions, feel free to reach out! And don't forget to let me know when you get engaged to Mr. Perfect-for-You!

devorahkigel.com
@devorahkigel
Devorah Rose Kigel (FB)
Devorah Kigel (YouTube)
devorahkigel@gmail.com

Chapter 1

Preparing to Meet Mr. Perfect-for-You

Welcome to your crash course in finding *the one*! If you're reading this, you're probably sick of dating by now, and you're wondering why you haven't found Mr. Perfect and settled down for your wonderful life together. Believe me, I know how *that* feels.

My own dating life was a complete disaster until I figured out a few very important things, which I can't wait to share with you.

But first, let's get things straight. There is no Mr. Perfect! *No human is perfect.* If you're holding out for perfection, ladies, you're going to be waiting for a *very long time*. Instead, we're going to work on finding Mr. Perfect-for-You – the one guy who has everything you *need*, even if he doesn't have everything you *want*. But guess what: if you're clear on what you really *need*, you never have to settle.

My hope for you as we embark on this journey together is that at the right time (very soon), you'll be writing to let me know that you've met him at last. Your soulmate! (Please send engagement pics!) I work as a dating coach and Jewish educator, and it gives me so much pleasure to hear your news.

Now, let's get started on what we need to do to get to your happy day.

Date Yourself First

Before we rush out to meet another guy who may or may not be compatible with you, we need to slow down and step back. Before we jump into dating *other people,* we actually need to date ourselves.

(Ok, maybe not *literally* – although if you want to do this at a coffee shop, that's fine with me.) It might sound cliché, but I cannot know who I'm compatible with if I don't know myself first.

When it comes to knowing myself, there are a lot of things to figure out. For example, what are my core values and beliefs? What are my life goals? How do I feel about Judaism? How do I want to raise my children? What are my values about finances and being a stay-at-home mother versus working outside the home? We want to have a clear idea of all this stuff before we start looking for the guy who's going to be our partner in life. Sometimes journaling is a good way to explore these issues.

But beyond the answers to those typical questions, we also want to have an idea of our unique strengths and weaknesses.

In Judaism, marriage is viewed as two souls reuniting. The first human being was actually created as a man and a woman joined together (Genesis 1:27). This being looked around at all the other creations that had mates, felt lonely, and requested a partner. So God separated them and formed Eve from Adam's rib (Genesis 2:22). When he met her, he felt that strange sense we feel when we get to know our husband-to-be. We feel we're finding the person who has something we're missing. It's like he is "bone of my bones, and flesh of my flesh" (Genesis 2:23) – a part of me that I've been looking for.

It's a little bit like a jigsaw puzzle. I have a little hole somewhere in me, and he also has a little hole in him, and I want to find the person who fits into my missing space and whose missing space I fit into. I have to ask myself, *what kinds of qualities will complement me?* Which means I have to know where I'm weak, so I can find a guy who is strong in those areas.

But I want you to turn it around also. Think about where you are strong. What are your unique special traits? What do you excel at? You want to look for a guy who's a great person and has a lot of good qualities, but who specifically needs what you have to bring to the table. Because if you and he are strong in the same ways, then life's not as interesting.

I'll give you an example. I'm a big personality, occasionally to a fault. And the woman my husband dated before me was really tame. You know, a really, really nice American girl. My husband is Russian, by the way. So she was just…so nice. And she would say to him, "Wow, you're so great. Everything you do is so great."

Guess what? He broke up with her. Because he said to himself, *If I marry this girl, I'm never going to fulfill my potential and get off the couch.* And then he married me, because he knew that he would become the greatest version of himself that way.

So even though I can be a bit…direct at times (there's always a downside to every virtue), my strengths were what he needed. He was looking for a woman who had that trait of being very ambitious and a go-getter, because he knew he wanted to acquire that trait for himself.

Sometimes we might make the mistake of thinking we want someone who is exactly the same as us. Let's face it, we like our own good qualities. But really it makes more sense to complement each other. We need shared goals and values, for sure, but identical personalities and strengths, no.

Ok, we're one step closer to figuring out who Mr. Perfect-for-You is: you need to know yourself and your strengths and weaknesses, so that you'll know what kind of person will complement you.

Figure Out Your Deal-Breakers

Once you've spent some time getting to know yourself a bit better, it's time to start figuring out what you need in Mr. Perfect-for-You. And if you're like most of us, you probably have a whole laundry list of the things you want. *Tall, dark, and handsome*, anyone? *Cool? Charming? Has a super-successful career? Always knows the right thing to say to make me feel like a million bucks?*

We all have stuff that we fantasize about or have seen in the movies that we would just *love* to find in a guy. And if Mr. Perfect-for-You has got that stuff, great! But most of the time, he is not going to have all those things on your laundry list, all the little preferences that we dream about…

For instance, since I'm fluent in French, I really wanted a French guy. And I also kind of wanted a Sephardi guy, because I feel like I'm a Sephardi soul trapped in an Ashkenazi body. Okay, so I thought, I want a French-speaking Sephardi guy, right?

Guess what? I married an Ashkenazi Russian guy. My French Sephardi fantasy was a preference. It was not a need.

In order to find our husband, we're going to have to cut down our shopping list…a lot. And we have to focus on the things that we really *need* and not just all the stuff that we *want*. We want to be discerning, not picky. So give some real thought to what your absolute needs are.

You know what was one of my needs? Someone who's a super-positive person, with an easygoing personality and no anger issues. Now, which do you think is more important? Sephardi French guy? Or positive, calm person? It's a good thing I got all of my needs and not all of my wants!

Needs are things that are *essential* for your happiness and fulfillment, whereas wants usually come from either peer pressure, the media, or more superficial stuff. The process of clarifying your *needs* is called making your deal-breaker list. Let's get started!

Making a Deal-Breaker List

Your deal-breaker list is *the most critical thing* to enable you to date smart and marry the right person. It is my *most* important tool in coaching. You may have made lists in the past, but this is going to be different. The deal-breaker list will consist of approximately ten things that are NON-NEGOTIABLE. You CAN'T COMPROMISE on them. You could have a separate preference list if you want. But that's not your deal-breaker list.

What goes on the deal-breaker list?

Negatives – Airborne Peanut Allergies

Negatives. These are the things that you simply cannot live with. I call them "airborne peanut allergies." These are the personality traits and character traits that you can't even be in the same room with, because you have a visceral negative reaction to them.

For me, when a man raises his voice, I have an allergic reaction to it. Okay, I cannot be married to a man who has a temper. And in over two decades, it's only a handful of times my husband has raised his voice. That's pretty good. Everyone gets frustrated sometimes. But I am ALLERGIC to a man who has a temper or who is very critical.

That doesn't mean that a guy who raises his voice or is critical isn't marriageable. Another girl might not have these allergies. It's just that *I* couldn't marry a guy like that. Your deal-breaker list is totally unique to you.

Positives – My Must-Haves

Then you have the positives. These are the must-haves, the "deal-makers." These are the character and personality traits that are so crucial for you that you can't imagine spending your life with someone who doesn't have them.

You can list around five negatives and around five positives, or you can list only negatives or only positives – it doesn't matter. Some people can think more clearly with negatives – I know what I'm allergic to. And some people like to emphasize the positives.

You can go above ten items on your list if you must, but keep it to no more than twelve or thirteen items total. The main thing is not to have a laundry list of a million things; as long as the items on your list are true needs that either you cannot live with or you must have, it's good.

This list is going to be your GPS instructions for how to find your husband. It will keep you focused on what is truly important to you and whether the guy you're dating is *the one*.

Here are some samples of deal-breaker lists from some of my clients:[1]

Marissa's Deal-Breaker List	Ariela's Deal-Breaker List
Positives • Outgoing • Trustworthy • Passionate about Judaism • Growth-oriented • Ambitious/driven • Zest for life • Open-minded	**Positives** • Intelligent • Empathetic/understanding • Sense of humor • Confident • Adventurous • Family-oriented • Passionate • Honest/has integrity
Negatives/Allergies • Anger • Negativity • Unhealthy communication • Smoker	**Negatives/Allergies** • Too frugal/cheap • Needy • Critical • Dishonest • Superficial

What If I Get Stuck?

If you're having trouble coming up with your list, there are a few things that might help. Think about your family of origin. Just like with a peanut allergy, you don't know you're allergic to it until you have a first exposure. So you want to think about your family, think about your father, your mother, siblings – what were you exposed to? Do you have any "allergies" because of how you grew up?

Next, you want to think about your dating history. Why did you break up with so-and-so even though he seemed like a great guy and had a lot of what you were looking for? Maybe it's because he had a trait that you're allergic to.

---

1   Note that all client names and details have been changed to protect privacy.

You can also think about friends of yours. Why do you connect with certain friends, while others kind of irritate you?

Money is another thing to think about. And I don't mean how much money the guy has – because that's something that can change. More relevant is his attitude toward money. And this is really subjective. Being offensive when you're drunk or angry is kind of an objective red flag. But money is very subjective. One person might be okay with someone who's very careful with money, and that doesn't bother her. And for another person, it's an allergy.

So you have to know yourself and figure out – is this a deal-breaker or not? I know people who are happily married to men who are super careful with money, and the wife doesn't care. But if my husband were checking my receipts after I went to the mall and telling me to return stuff, I think I would go out of my mind! For me, that's an allergy.

The other important thing is that you have to be *specific* in the stuff that you write. Don't write "nice." Or for my religious girls, "good *middos*" (positive character traits). Stop – there are thousands of good character traits in the world. You can't have them all!

So which part of "nice" is the most important thing for you? It could be he's a good listener. It could be he's compassionate. It could be he does good deeds for other people. It could be he is very empathetic. There are so many different aspects of nice! So don't write "nice" or "good character." I want you to pick out the few highly specific character traits that *for you* are most crucial.

What about Physical Traits?

Here's a little warning. You're not allowed to put physical traits on your deal-breaker list! I forbid it!

Okay, did I say you should marry someone you're not attracted to? No! For obvious reasons, Judaism mandates marrying someone you're attracted to – there's a law that the couple must see each other before agreeing to get married. As a dating coach, I never let my clients marry without attraction. So you *will be attracted* to the guy you marry.

But you can't decide in advance that you will never be attracted to a guy who is *dark, light, tall, short, blue-eyed, brown-eyed,* whatever! Specific physical traits should not be written on your list. I always say, we want to leave God open to His magic – sometimes He puts your bashert into a package you wouldn't have envisioned.

I once helped a girl who was five foot one, and she said, "He must be over six feet." I told her, "First of all, that's like three Jewish guys! LOL. And secondly, you're five one! What are you thinking? We are not writing that down."

You will know if you're attracted to your husband before you get married. And the truth is, sometimes we have a mental picture of what our husband is going to look like – our "type." And we often end up marrying someone very different from that picture. He might be a little shorter. He might be losing his hair. He might have glasses, or whatever. We don't want to be a stickler about physicality. Give the guy a chance and focus on his character. If everything else fits, attraction will often click into place.

And by the way, I like to say that it's much easier to fix muscles than *middos.*

Meaning, the physical stuff can be worked on (as long as he's open to it). You don't like his style? Take him shopping. Don't like his teeth? Have him see a dentist. Don't like his weight? He can work out. But the inside stuff is hard to change. So don't get hung up on externals.

Jewish Red Lines

One last thing, while you're coming up with your deal-breaker list. As you figure out the positive and negative traits that you need, it's a good idea to also clarify what I call your "Jewish red lines."

This means how far to the right or the left you would be willing to go in terms of the guy's Judaism. If you're religious, your red lines might be that the guy keeps kosher, keeps Shabbat, and wears a kippah. If you're even more religiously observant, the red lines might include that he studies Torah or prays every day. Maybe you're not as focused on actual religious practice, and a red line is just that he's Jewish? Or that he fasts on Yom Kippur?

Whatever these red lines are, it's important to get them on paper before you start dating. Get clarity *before* you meet the guy – don't try to decide what's important after you've met him and gotten emotionally involved.

You Can Have It All – If You Do It Right!

Like I said, this list is going to be your GPS instructions on how to find your husband.

If you've really only put needs on your list, it's completely realistic to get everything on your deal-breaker list, as long as your needs are real and *reasonable*. If you need advice on whether your deal-breaker list is reasonable, bring it to a dating coach or a happily married (not single…) friend and see what your trusted advisor says.

Basically, we never have to compromise on what's truly important to us. Settling is not something ANY of my clients have done, no matter what age they were.

Arianna's Story

Arianna came from a family that was pressuring her to get married. Her parents kept trying to convince her to re-date one of the guys she had turned down in the past. "Why are you so picky?" they would say. "You're never going to get married! He was such a nice boy!"

So Arianna, who wants to please her family, starts to think, *Maybe I am being too picky? Maybe I shouldn't have said no?* Enter the deal-breaker list. I sat down with her, and we went through her deal-breakers. Turns out, this really nice guy was missing half of her non-negotiables! She did not need to be second-guessing herself about saying no!

So that's another benefit of the deal-breaker list. It gives you the clarity and confidence to explain to your loved ones and matchmakers why you broke off a relationship or are not interested in dating someone.

How Else Should I Prepare?

We're going to talk about what you can do with your deal-breaker list a bit later. In the meantime, we're working on making you as ready for marriage as you can be.

We talked about knowing yourself. And we talked about figuring out what you really, truly need in a husband.

What else can you do to get ready for marriage?

Learn to Be Others-Centered

We want to learn to be others-centered. Marriage, and subsequently having kids, is all about giving, giving, and giving some more. Now, hopefully, your husband is also giving, but your kids for sure aren't giving back until much, much later. So you want to really exercise this muscle of being a giving person.

> **Handy Hebrew Helper:** *Chesed* is the Hebrew word used to describe loving-kindness. It refers to giving to other people in an expansive way. It's important to get in the habit of giving, because once you get married (soon!), you're going to be doing a lot of it!

You can do this in so many different ways. Consider doing some form of *chesed* – volunteering, visiting people in the hospital, cooking a meal for someone who just had a baby, holding someone's baby while she takes care of her other kids... Even just paying attention to a host and offering to set or clear the table or make food is a good way to get practice. Just try, in some way, to make sure that your monthly schedule includes some form of giving to other people.

Work on Your Self-Esteem

Many women struggle with this. We aren't going to be able to date from a place of confidence, objectivity, clarity, and dignity if we don't love ourselves. If you're the type to get kind of desperate and to latch onto anything that seems like interest or love from a guy, even if he's only giving you "breadcrumbs," it's time to work on self-love. If you find yourself in the habit of dating guys who don't treat you with respect or who put you down, you probably need to work on self-esteem.

If you know you have healing to do, you might want to do some therapy before you're ready to date seriously. Sometimes, it might be enough to read self-help books. Obviously, the healthier we are when we're dating, the healthier our decisions – and later our marriages – will be.

Don't Press Pause on Your Life

Here's another thing about dating. If I told you right now that you're going to meet your husband six months from now, how would you spend the next six months? You would have so much fun, right? You'd be so relaxed. You would just take the next six months and enjoy yourself, travel, take time for hobbies, spend time with friends…

Sometimes, when we're dating, we sort of "press pause" on our life. We're waiting. I'm not going to decorate my apartment because what if I get married? I don't want to travel because what if I meet someone? I don't want to sign up for this art class because I want to be uber-available for dating. And I don't want to sign up for a gym membership because what if I end up moving when I meet the right guy?

None of this makes sense. We want to be present in the moment that we're in. Dive into your life and enjoy every aspect of single life. Devote yourself to your learning and growth – learn a new language, take cooking classes, travel, hang out with girlfriends, go to a Torah class, go to Israel – there are so many things you could do for yourself and your personal growth that you will not be able to do once you're married with kids. Seriously, as a wife and mother of young kids, if you get five minutes to yourself, it's like *wow, what a good day!* That's just the way it is. So enjoy the present. Don't press pause on your life.

And then when you do go on a date, you'll have much more to share; you'll be so much more interesting, lively, and happy because you're filling yourself up instead of pressing pause. By the way, this applies to all stages of life. When you're newly married, enjoy that stage! Go out for date night (before you need babysitters!). Do stuff with just your husband. Then when you have kids, enjoy that stage. Be in the *now*.

Stay Optimistic

Ladies, I know, this is SO hard. When we date for a long time, it is so easy to get bitter and discouraged. You're like, *If I go on one more annoying date…you know what, forget it! I'll just be single for the rest of my life. It's fine, I'll get a cat!* You start to expect all your dates to be DOA (dead on arrival).

By the time I met my husband, I was so…done. After so many frogs, it was really hard to be hopeful about meeting my prince! But even though it's challenging to remain optimistic, it's worth it.

If I could pinpoint the one thing that my successfully married clients have in common, it's a sense of optimism and hope – of being open to the possibility that this time could be different.

So give a guy a chance. We always have to be respectful to someone. Even if you know within the first five minutes that this guy's not for you, still, we have to be courteous.

The other thing that can happen when we've been dating a while is that we start thinking about settling – marrying someone we're not really attracted to or excited about.

I want you to work on shifting your mindset here – *even though I've been dragged through the mud, I'm going to value myself, value my time, stick to my deal-breaker list, and have faith that there is a person out there who is uniquely suited to me.*

Every one of my clients was excited about who they were marrying, regardless of whether they were twenty-five, thirty-five, forty-five, fifty-five, or sixty-five! They did not feel they were set-tling. You deserve to marry someone who fulfills your core values and has the traits that you need. So believe in yourself!

Is it easy to stay positive? No, it's really not easy. Especially when you've been looking for a long time. And you don't have to be *completely* there. I was still pretty pessimistic when I met my husband. To be honest, on every date that I went on with my husband, I was waiting for the other shoe to drop. Thank God, the other shoe never dropped!

You don't have to be completely healed from your experiences in order to get married. You just have to be open and give things a chance.

It's fine to "fake it 'til you make it." Think positive thoughts and smile. Always try to keep the bitterness in check and put your best foot forward. Remember, God has someone picked out for you. Statistics, numbers, and doom-and-gloom articles are irrele-vant. As my mother always used to tell me, "You only need one."

No Such Thing as Wasted Time

Finally, it's also important to remember that if you are serious and putting your best effort into your dating, there's no such thing as wasted time. I know that dating can start to feel like we're just spinning our wheels. But it does not have to be so.

As long as you are learning something from each experience, then every wrong date is just another stepping stone on your way to meeting your husband. Try journaling and making a list of the take-away lessons you've learned, so you can benefit from them. Think about what each experience is teaching you. Maybe it highlighted the importance of a particular deal-breaker for you? Maybe it taught you something about what you need that you weren't previously aware of. One of my favorite lines is "Focus on the repair, not the despair."

And if the guy who isn't for you is a nice guy, you can always think about whether you have a friend you can set him up with. You know, if he's five two and you're five eight, you have no idea why anyone thought that was a good idea. But you have a friend who's five one, and maybe they'd be good for each other, or perhaps you're not on the same page religiously, but you have a friend he'd be perfectly aligned with? Matches are made this way all the time, and it's a big mitzvah! We've got to find the potential positive in every experience.

Use Your Higher Power

One last thing…or maybe it should be the first thing. We're going to talk about all the stuff you have to do to try to find *the one*. But at the end of the day, you can't control where he comes from. You can't *force* the universe to send him to you.

Handy Hebrew Helper: A mitzvah actually means a commandment, but it's used colloquially to mean a good deed. Basically, it's an action that is aligned with God's will.

So whatever you do to get a little spiritual – whether you pray, meditate, visualize, or manifest – use it here. Try to connect to the Higher Power in the universe and ask for the help you need to meet your match. Ancient Jewish sources teach that forty days before a baby is born, a voice from Heaven calls out: *this boy will marry this girl*. So, I firmly believe that God has someone perfect-for-you picked out.

Chapter 2

The Ingredients of a Great Marriage

N ow that we've gotten through some of the preparatory steps, let's get into what the ingredients are for a great marriage.

In the last chapter, we talked a little about you *individually*. To get married, you have to know yourself, and you have to know what you need in your husband.

But what about marriage in *general*? What qualities, across the board, do we need to find if we want to succeed at making it work with someone for the next twenty, thirty, forty, fifty, sixty, even seventy years of our lives? Marriage is not easy, even if you do marry the right person. But with the right qualities and the right attitudes, it is totally possible to have a fantastic marriage.

So what are the ingredients that we need for a good, lasting marriage? What are the things you should be looking for in a spouse, and what should you be working on in yourself?

The Four G's

Author Gila Manolson talks about the Three *G*'s.[1] Look for a guy who is giving, good, and into growth. And I'm going to add a fourth *G* to that list: gratitude. This means across the board for everyone, regardless of your deal-breaker list, you want to look for a guy who has these qualities.

Why? Well, if a guy has a good heart, or *lev tov*, it means he's a mensch and wants to make you happy. And if he's giving,

---

1   See among her other books Gila Manolson, *Head to Heart: What to Know before Dating and Marriage* (Nanuet: Feldheim, 2002).

> **Handy Hebrew Helper:** *Lev tov* technically means "good heart" in Hebrew. The sages speak about it as a good trait that is kind of all-encompassing. For our purposes, it refers to a person who's kind and really wants to do the right thing and make you happy.

he's ready for the work of marriage and family, which is about giving much of the time.

But what happens when his intentions are good but he's not aware of your "love language" or has a hard time knowing how to validate when you're upset? If he's growth-oriented, you'll talk about it, and he'll try to change. And you'll grow and figure stuff out together. Or he'll speak to his mentor/rabbi/therapist to get some tips on how to do better. But if he's not growth-oriented, he's not going to want to learn.

For marriage to be successful, it's crucial to marry a growth-oriented person. Which means you want to hear *while you're dating* that he has a growth mindset. He's learning new stuff. He likes to go to this class or listen to that podcast; he's reading a book on relationships or on maximizing potential or whatever. Basically, anything that shows you that he wants to improve himself, and he knows he doesn't have all the answers.

> **Handy Hebrew Helper:** *Hakarat hatov* literally means "recognizing the good" in Hebrew. Having an awareness of the good is what we call in English "gratitude."

Note to self: Don't settle for promises. Actions speak louder than words. You must see him *currently* taking steps to get to his stated goals.

My fourth *G* is gratitude. In Hebrew, it's called *hakarat hatov*, which means having an awareness of the good. Why is gratitude important? It's a very foundational point in marriage. If you cannot express appreciation to someone else, it's going to be a rough ride. Generally, one of the most common complaints I hear from married women is a lack of appreciation on the part of their husbands.

So pay attention when you hear him talking. Does he express appreciation for the people in his life? When you bake him some cookies or do something for him, does he acknowledge it in detail? Does he stop at "Yeah, thanks." Or is he more expressive: "Wow, that was so thoughtful of you. Chocolate chip is my favorite kind!" A man who is grateful will be happier himself and have a happier wife (you!) as well. So be on the lookout for this quality.

Open to Mentorship

We already know he needs to match our deal-breaker list. And we know he needs to be giving, good-hearted, growth-oriented, and have gratitude. But that's still not enough.

We also really want a husband who can humble himself to a mentor. If he's religious, this will be a rabbi. Otherwise, it could be a therapist, a dating coach, an older family member, or a married friend who coaches him on things. Whoever it is, the important thing is that he's willing to take advice from other people and implement it.

I unfortunately get too many phone calls from married women who tell me a whole sad saga of marital troubles. And the first question I ask them is, "Is there anyone your husband will listen to? Therapist, rabbi, friend…anyone?" And often the answer is no. What can I tell a wife like that? Pray?

If your husband is the type of man who refuses to humble himself to get guidance, then he thinks he knows it all. You're thinking, *Oh, my gosh, we really need someone to help us out with this issue.* And meanwhile, he's saying, "What do you mean? I don't need to talk to anyone. I know what I'm doing!" This is a recipe for disaster.

Differences of opinion, arguments, and disagreements about major life choices WILL come up during a marriage. Period. Full stop. I mean, this is the rest of your life we're talking about – it's normal to have some conflict in relationships.

When we're single, we can make independent decisions without having to take into account another person's preferences and needs. But when you're married, there is someone else there. And what happens when you guys go head to head and just cannot agree? Being able to speak to an objective party is super important in these moments. If the guy you're dating is not the kind of person who is willing to do this, I can guarantee there will be big problems in your marriage.

So if you see that he has no mentor and isn't willing to even look for one, it's a big red flag.

Foundation of Friendship

We've touched on several of the key traits that it's important for each of you, individually, to have in a marriage. Both of you are working on the four *G*'s, and ideally you should both have a mentor or someone you would go to for advice.

Now I want to talk about the things that need to be a part of your relationship with each other. The stuff we've talked about so far was sort of like finding quality ingredients – you're each great people on your own. And these next points are about how the flavors combine into the perfect recipe – whether the two of you *together* have what it takes for a great marriage.

The first thing that you want to have with the guy you marry is *friendship*.

Huh? Friendship? Isn't marriage about romance?

Actually, wrong. According to Jewish wisdom, the basis of a great marriage is friendship. The sixth and seventh of the Sheva Berachot, the seven blessings recited during the marriage ceremony, refer to the couple as *re'im ha'ahuvim* (loving friends) and wish them, "exultation, delight, amusement and pleasure, love and brotherhood, peace and friendship." This means that your husband should eventually become your best friend. I call this the foundation of friendship, and it refers to the fact that the person you're dating should start becoming part of your inner circle if he's the right one.

As you date longer, he gradually becomes the address you want to turn to when you're feeling a bit down, or something funny happened at work that you want to share, or you want to tell someone about your great achievement or a conflict with a coworker or friend. Talking to him might not be the same as with your BFF or your sister (we still need our girlfriends!), but if he's the right guy, eventually you'll enjoy speaking to him about what's happening in your life.

One of the things you should notice as you date longer is that *it just feels good to be with him.* You like being in his presence. You don't have to be talking – you could just be walking next to each other in the park. And you like that feeling. You feel safe. You don't feel awkward. You laugh together. You just feel really good.

You want to make sure you have fun with him doing…nothing. Because most of life is a lot of nothing. It's groceries, bills, the mortgage, the kids, diapers, all these types of things. It's a lot of mundane. So you better have fun with this person while you're dealing with the mundane stuff of life.

This is why you want to make sure that your dating period is not all super-exciting stuff. I was once dating a wealthy guy, and he took me to Broadway shows and fancy restaurants and so on. After a month of dating him, it suddenly occurred to me, *Hmm…do I like* him *or do I like Manhattan?* It ended up being Manhattan!

Instead, to see if that foundation of friendship is there, you want to make sure that a lot of the dating process is just kind of walking around and talking. You know what I mean? He's not whisking you off to Paris – everything isn't off-the-charts exciting. You're just talking and getting to know each other, and you're really enjoying being with him.

If things aren't over the top and you still enjoy being with him, and he makes you laugh, you will start to notice that foundation of friendship gradually sneaking up on you. If he matches your deal-breaker list and the friendship is developing, then ladies, we are looking at a promising situation.

Shared Goals and Values

What else does your relationship need if it's going to succeed long-term? Super important point here: shared goals and values. You cannot *not* talk about this stuff.

Please do not wait until three months into the relationship to talk about your attitude toward Judaism, or how you want your home to be, or your approach to finances – these are big things, and sometimes they're even deal-breakers.

Examples of areas you may wish to explore, for example, might include the following:

- What types of schools would you want to send your kids to (public versus day school or yeshiva)?
- Do you prefer to live in an urban environment or a smaller town?
- Do you love hosting guests or do you prefer a quieter life?
- What type of lifestyle and standard of living do you envision for yourself ten years from now?

Yes, marrying someone is about finding someone you connect with, someone you like, someone who makes you feel complete. But it's also about building a family and a home together. And when you build something with another person, you had better be on the same page about what you're trying to build. Even small differences in values and goals will magnify once you have children.

So talk about these things! For example, if you want to see if you're aligned in terms of how you relate to Judaism, one good way to figure this out is to ask, "What do you want Shabbat to be like in your home? What are the kids doing? Are we on our phones? Are our phones off? Are you giving a *d'var Torah*? What are we doing Friday night? Are we doing the next day also? What's going on?" That can kind of give you a picture of your future goals in this area and reveal whether the two of you have similar visions.

Handy Hebrew Helper: *A d'var Torah* literally means "a word of the Torah" in Hebrew. This refers to a brief discussion about a point in Torah that is relevant to the events of the day or to the gathering at which it is being said, such as a family celebration or on Shabbat and holidays.

Another thing to talk about is your attitude toward the wife working outside the home while having kids. Most of the women I talk to, regardless of religiosity, and even if they have very high-powered careers, still want to feel that their husbands are going to take financial responsibility. And that's a valid conversation to have. You could say to him, "You know, even though I'm a [fill in the blank: accountant, banker, lawyer, doctor, teacher, whatever], I don't know how I'm going to feel once I have babies. I might decide I want to stay home and raise them myself. How do you feel about that? Is that something you'd be supportive of?"

And if his reaction is "What?! I can't do that!" or "That's a big responsibility!" – it might be an immediate no. Or maybe it's a conversation. Maybe you want to see how he feels about moving somewhere more affordable to live. Maybe you could work part-time. But at least you've begun the important conversations about values.

You also want to figure out if you're aligned in how you make financial decisions in general. Do you pay your credit card bill on time? Do you carry a lot of debt? Do you not care? Do you spend money on things versus experiences? Again, it's not wrong for him to be one way or another. What's important is that the two of you are on the same page or at least facing in the same direction, you feel confident that you can work together, and you see that your core values are aligned.

So please don't push off the conversations about goals and values. Don't get all emotionally involved with someone and then realize down the line that you're on a totally different page. That's just not smart.

Emotional Intimacy

Moving along in our recipe for a good relationship, the next ingredient is emotional intimacy.

What is emotional intimacy? Well, how do you feel around this guy? Do you feel safe? Can you be honest about who you are? Can you share the things you struggle with? Do you feel cared for, seen, and accepted by him? Over time, are you starting to feel deeply connected?

Emotional intimacy with a guy is similar to what it might be with a very close friend. Does it feel like he is the person you would eventually want to tell personal things to? Do you feel a kind of warmth with him? Do you feel safe and secure in his presence?

Now, emotional intimacy develops for different people in different ways. Some people have an easy time feeling emotionally close to someone. Others take a while to open up and get close. While emotional intimacy could be something that just comes automatically over the course of your dating process (not right away, but little by little), some people might get stuck before getting to emotional intimacy.

We will talk about this more, but for now I want to say that just because you don't automatically feel emotionally close doesn't mean you should break up with a guy. Sometimes we do have to work at it a little bit – like by paying attention to when we feel close to a guy and trying to do more of the activities that help us feel close.

Maybe it's having deep conversations and being vulnerable. Or going on fun outings. Sometimes we can build emotional intimacy through giving – like getting him a small gift, something you know he likes, or baking him cookies. I know baking cookies is so cliché, but it comes from this warm, feminine side that can be really helpful at bringing the two of you closer.

Either way, by the time you stand under the chuppah, the emotional intimacy piece definitely needs to be there. If you're having trouble with it, talk to a mentor or do any of the things I suggested. But you definitely should not get married if you don't feel emotionally connected.

Mutual Respect

On the one hand, you need to feel admiration and respect for him. One of my clients said she asked herself, *If our kids turned out basically like him, would I be happy?* On the other hand, do you feel he treats you and speaks to you respectfully? Or does he steamroll you? Talk over you? Argue and try to change your opinion? Invalidate your ideas? Put you down? Criticize you a lot? Those are big red flags. Ultimately, guys will treat you as well or as badly as you allow them to, so if we've dated guys who don't treat us respectfully, we need to examine our part in that.

Yes, respect is something that you will work on throughout your marriage. But based on what you know and appreciate about the guy from the start, you should naturally feel a certain respect for him and vice versa. Relationships where either side doesn't respect the other get toxic super quickly. Mutual respect is completely essential for a marriage.

Attraction

Drumroll, ladies! The thing we've all been waiting to discuss… attraction!

Yes, attraction is absolutely a necessary ingredient for a successful marriage. But before you start piling your deal-breaker list a mile high with all the ways you want him to look (I don't allow that, remember?), let's talk about what we really mean by attraction.

First of all, we want to distinguish between chemistry and attraction. Chemistry is where you walk into that singles event, you see him across the room, you lock eyes, and it's like, *crackle, crackle* – there's electricity going through the sound waves. Instant fireworks. You have not spoken. You have no idea who he is. He could be a complete jerk. A total disaster. He could say something completely offensive. He could be brain-dead. But you're just like, *crackle, crackle*, right? (*Let's see if I can "accidentally" bump into him so we can meet!*) That's chemistry, and let's be clear that we do not want to base any decisions on chemistry!

What's attraction? It doesn't have to be immediate – the more you get to know him, the cuter he appears to you. Maybe on the first date, you're kind of neutral, but by date number three, you start to think, *He's just so sweet.* And then the next date, you're feeling kind of excited and thinking, *Oh, my gosh, we had such a great conversation! He's so cute!* And he just becomes more and more attractive, the more you get to know his good qualities and the more you're connecting on an emotional level.

Now, when it comes to actually noticing whether we feel attracted to a guy, it kind of depends on who you are.

If you're the type of person who is easily infatuated, you should probably hold yourself back a little bit and make sure to lead with your head. Think of yourself almost like a newspaper reporter. Does he match my deal-breaker list? Do we have common goals and values? Does he have good character? Really try to lead with your brain and then check things with your heart afterwards. Your heart *does* have to be on board by the end, but it shouldn't necessarily be leading the parade.

If you're the opposite – the super-logical type of person who tends to overthink things – then you want to make sure your heart is part of the process. Be present in your body. Think about how you feel when you're with him. Do you feel like being close to him? Do you feel safe? Do you feel comfortable? Do you laugh together? Does he make eye contact? Get in touch with your heart and your body.

You have to be attracted to the person you spend your life with, a hundred percent. And if you are grossed out by a guy, I would never tell you to even go on a second date with him! At the same time, we want our feelings to be based on real attraction, which stems from seeing his good qualities and experiencing how he treats us. If it's just sexual chemistry, and he's not treating you with respect, this is not going to be a good marriage. You need to leave the situation now.

My mentor who trained me, Rosie Einhorn, a therapist and dating coach, says that for women, physical attraction is mostly about eyes and smile. He doesn't have to be the perfect physical specimen or "the type" that you had in your mind. But you think his eyes are gorgeous. If you think he has a beautiful smile, and you have a fantastic time with him, and all the other things are lining up – don't break up with that, just because you don't feel attracted to him yet.

We need to give attraction time to develop. It's like the stock market. There could be dates that are a little up and down in the attraction department. But as long as the general progression is up, there's enough potential to continue.

* * *

So there we have it! The ingredients for a successful marriage:

1. Four *G*'s: good, giving, growth-oriented, and grateful
2. Has a mentor
3. Foundation of friendship

4. Shared goals and values
5. Emotional intimacy
6. Mutual respect
7. And attraction!

Now that we've discussed the foundations, we're ready to start looking for guys to date!

Chapter 3

Getting Ready to Date

O kay. I've "dated myself," I have my deal-breaker list, and I even have a good, grounded idea of the qualities I'm going to need for a good marriage.

But wait…how do I meet guys? How do I get dates? That is going to be the first topic we address in this chapter.

And then, once I meet someone, or get set up with someone, how do I find out whether he's got what I need or not?

For example, my clients ask me, "How do I know if he has a temper? If he's really a respectful person or he's just trying to impress me? And how do I know if he matches my deal breaker list?"

And I respond that it's a little like doing a color-by-number picture. Remember when you were little, you did those pictures with lots of shapes, and each shape had a number in it that you were supposed to color in with a certain color?

Well, dating is a lot like a color-by-number. You start off with a black outline of a bunch of shapes – the dating resume, the description on the dating app, or how someone described him to you – and you're not really sure what you're looking at. What kind of guy is he? Do I like him? Does he match my deal-breakers list? What are his values?

You're not going to get the answers to all that stuff at once. As you get to know him, you will slowly color in a few of those boxes. And then, if you date him long enough, the other little shapes will gradually get colored in, and you'll start to see the whole picture.

If I know how to get information and what kind of information to look for, I'm going to be able to fill in more of those shapes earlier on. Getting that kind of information is our second topic for this chapter.

Finally, no dating process should be embarked upon alone! No, you don't need to bring a friend along on your dates, but you do want someone objective to help you make smart decisions. That's why – either before you start dating or early in the process – it's good to choose a dating mentor. That will be our last topic for this chapter.

Getting Dates

Some of you might not have a problem with finding people to date. Some of you may struggle to get suggestions or get asked out. No matter what, we all want to work on how we get dates, because the smarter we are about it, the more likely we are to get dates with the kind of guy we're actually looking for.

Write Your Deal-Breaker Blurb

How do we go about getting dates with suitable guys? Remember your deal-breaker list with around ten items of your absolutely essential needs? We're going to take that list and use it to make "the blurb." The blurb is essentially your deal-breaker list in sentence form. It doesn't have to have everything on your list, but it should cover most of it. Basically, it's a two- or three-sentence description of what you're looking for.

Let's look again for example at Marissa's deal-breaker list.

Marissa's Deal-Breaker List
Positives
Outgoing
Trustworthy
Passionate about Judaism
Growth-oriented

Ambitious/driven
Zest for life
Open-minded

Negatives/Allergies
Anger
Negativity
Unhealthy communication
Smoker

Based on her list, Marissa's blurb might read something like this:

> I'm looking for an outgoing guy who is passionate about Judaism. He should be growth-oriented, ambitious, and have a zest for life, but also open-minded. He cannot be prone to anger, negativity, or toxic communication patterns. He must also be a non-smoker.

Now you're going to use this blurb to help people around you know what kind of guy you're looking for.

For those of you making official dating profiles, you might put this on your "dating resume" or give it to a matchmaker to help people set you up with guys who are on target. And if you're on a dating site, it will often ask you to describe what you're looking for. So you'll put your blurb there.

And if you're not doing that type of official dating, it's just something that you might send out to someone who's a married friend, an acquaintance, or a mentor who likes to set people up. You'll just send this quick little paragraph, saying something like, "I just want to let you know that this is what I'm looking for. I'd love it if you could keep me in mind."

And believe me, ladies, people really *do* want to help. They might not know anyone, but if they do meet a guy who fits your description, how happy do you think they would be to let you know?

The Elevator Pitch

Next step – you're going to take your blurb, which is about three to four sentences, and you're going to distill it into one sentence. This sentence is your "elevator pitch."

An elevator pitch is what you'd say if the CEO of the company gets in the elevator with you and you're looking for a different job in the company. You have eight seconds as the elevator goes down to the lobby to explain to the CEO what kind of job you're looking for.

So you want to have an "elevator pitch" of your deal-breaker list. Eight seconds – write a sentence or two that encapsulates the most important things you're looking for.

Now, you're ready for the next time you go to a Shabbat meal, a work function, a networking event, a family gathering, or a community event, and someone comes up to you and says, "Hey, you're adorable. I would love to set you up. What are you looking for?" If you have time, you could say your whole blurb. But if you want to just get it off your tongue in a quick, efficient way, say your elevator pitch.

This will help people to set you up more successfully. Whether you're working with a formal matchmaker or just friends and family who are trying to help you find Mr. Right, if you can convey to them your deal-breaker list as an elevator pitch very quickly, it creates a mental picture for them of what you're looking for.

I'm not a matchmaker. I'm a dating coach. Matchmaking is just not my skillset. But there was one match that I made. The young woman said to me, "I'm looking for an NCSY camp counselor type." (NCSY is a religious Jewish youth group.)

I immediately pictured a big personality. Super fun, happy, funny – just a big, great personality. So then there was a guy who was dating one of my clients, and she ended it with him. I didn't even meet him, but I just heard her describe him. And I thought, *Oh, my gosh, it's the NCSY camp counselor!* Because I had this picture in my mind, I suggested the match to the other young woman. Thank God, they're married with two kids.

So your elevator pitch is about giving over the essentials of what you're looking for in a succinct manner.

Remember the deal-breaker lists we saw before? Here are the elevator pitches that might go with them:

Marissa's Elevator Pitch

I'm looking for someone open-minded and passionate about Judaism. He should be ambitious, trustworthy, and even-tempered.

Ariela's Elevator Pitch

I'm looking for an intelligent, empathetic, adventurous man who is honest, responsible, positive, and has a great sense of humor.

Sometimes, you might be able to distill what you're looking for into something even shorter and simpler – like the "NCSY camp counselor type" example. This is where you can use wording to create a mental picture that can turn on a light bulb in someone's head and help them understand exactly what you're looking for.

For example, if you're looking for a sensitive, intelligent, adventurous, nature-loving guy, you might say, "I'm looking for a sensitive, outdoorsy type." Or maybe you're looking for "a family man with a sense of humor," or "a Breslov/Carlebach guy with a successful job." True, these descriptions don't include all your deal-breakers. But they're *based on your deal-breakers* and are likely to trigger an image that may make it easier for people to set you up.

A last note on this: don't be afraid to be specific. Some of my clients get nervous to be specific because they think then people won't set them up or won't find what they're looking for. I actually think it's the opposite – the more generic your description, the more people will just draw a blank. But the more specific you can be about what you need, the more you create a mental picture that brings a real person to someone's mind.

Network, Network, Network

Once we have all of this – our deal-breaker list, our blurb, and our elevator pitch – we need to start networking. This means number one, if you're working with professional matchmakers, you send your blurb and your resume, along with possibly a picture of yourself (more on that later, in chapter 6), to describe what you're looking for.

Also send it to friends, contacts, family members, and random people you know, especially if they happen to know a lot of people. As we said, people are happy to help.

Now you have to follow up (*cough* – nag them) regularly. Ideally every month, you should circle back to the same people that you reached out to and say, "Hey, just checking in. Do you know anyone who you think might be a good fit for me?" I did this for my daughters. I reached out to the same matchmakers once every month or two. You have to be a little bit annoying. That's okay.

Now, people say to me, *I feel so desperate doing this. I don't want to!* Ladies, let's be frank: if it came to finding a new job, you would be getting out there, sending out your resume, networking and talking to anyone and everyone who might know someone in your profession. "Oh, your uncle's brother's cousin's friend works in this industry? Here's my resume. Can you pass it along?"

You would have zero shame doing this. But somehow, when it comes to our personal life, we feel awkward or desperate. Shift your mindset. Take the same mentality that you use for your career and use it for dating.

I really respect someone who is straightforward and confident about what they're looking for. And believe me, I've heard so many random stories about people getting set up. A family knew that a certain girl was looking, and then they hosted a guy from another state for a Shabbat meal and thought to set them up. Another young woman ended up marrying a young man who was suggested randomly by someone who never met either of the parties involved. You never know where he'll come from!

When you network and then follow up, it keeps you on people's radar. They're more likely to think of you when they meet someone new. So don't give up! Keep reaching out so you stay on their minds. Especially remember to contact your married friends, who are the most likely to be the ones to set you up successfully, since they know you well.

No matter what, putting in the effort pays off in the long run. In the Jewish world, we call this effort *hishtadlut*, which means "trying." We know that God runs the show, and we don't know how we're going to meet the right guy. But we still have to be practical and try to find him. Maybe someone will hear your blurb and send him your way. Or maybe you'll meet him in a different way entirely! Either way, doing the legwork is like planting your seeds. If you plant and plant and plant, eventually, something is gonna grow.

> **Handy Hebrew Helper:** *Hishtadlut* means "due diligence" in Hebrew. While the religious perspective recognizes that the results are in God's hands, we nevertheless must do our own *histadlut* – that is, put in our own effort to try to make things happen.

Online Dating – Use with Care

A lot of people ask how I feel about online dating. And of course, we all know a few people who met that way, so it's a great question.

Generally speaking, I prefer websites that have some accountability. For instance, the SawYouAtSinai brand, which has several other sites connected to it, doesn't allow clients to scroll through profiles. Rather, a matchmaker has access to profiles and sorts through them to suggest matches. Only after a matchmaker has suggested a potential date do both parties gain access to each other's profiles so they can decide whether to try going on a date. That means there's an intermediary who can help and who's going to hold people accountable.

I've told many a client when they've been treated badly by a guy that was suggested through one of these sites – either he was rude, or he didn't follow up, or he ghosted – "Tell the matchmaker!"

We don't just throw our hands up when a guy mistreats us. We are part of a sisterhood – we have to take care of each other! So if you've been treated badly by someone or he hasn't behaved like a mensch, you really *should* tell the matchmaker. These guys should not be on the sites.

I'm not as much a fan of the dating apps (Hinge, Jswipe, etc). I know there are married couples who met through them; however, these sites don't generally attract many marriage-minded guys. There's no accountability, so the guys who are on them don't tend to be serious. It's also time-consuming and can cause burnout. Often guys will text or message back and forth for weeks without asking you out – what a waste of time! You could try out the apps for a bit and see how you feel. But definitely use your description to be as selective as possible so that you weed out the guys who are not for you or who are not even serious. I recommend when someone reaches out to you from an app, right off the bat message him a couple questions that will weed out noncompatible people. For example, if you're looking for someone who keeps kosher, say, "Hey, just double-checking that you read my profile where I mentioned that I keep kosher and want to have a kosher home?" Often, people aren't reading carefully; just asking a quick follow-up question or two will save you time and disappointment.

Obviously, suggestions from a matchmaker who takes the time to get to know you – or from a friend – tend to be more on target than looking at an online profile, because you're going to be suggested guys who are compatible with your stated goals and values, including being marriage-minded.

Train Your Matchmaker

If you are dating through a matchmaker – whether through a site or in person – you might find that the matchmaker is not making suitable suggestions. What do you do if that's the case? Firstly, don't rush to replace the matchmaker. Try giving some feedback. Say, "Thank you so much for thinking of me. I really, really appreciate it. Can I give you a little feedback so that you could maybe know a little bit more what I'm looking for?"

And then describe something specific. As an example, you might say, "The last guy I dated was really quiet and shy, and I'm very much looking for someone with a confident, outgoing personality."

That's a good amount of feedback to give someone either on a site or in person. You want to be as specific as possible, in a nice way. At the same time, also give positive feedback about anything that was a good fit. For example, "It was really close in many ways – he had this, this, and this quality that I'm looking for. But there's one aspect that really is a deal-breaker for me."

If you find, after a while, that none of the matches seem appropriate, it might be time to find a different matchmaker. Give the current matchmaker a chance, but if you do have to switch, there is no shame in that.

Getting Information

Okay, so we've covered a little bit about getting dates and the sites and people that are sometimes involved in that. Now we want to talk information. Someone has been suggested to you, and you have *no idea* what kind of person he is or whether he's appropriate. What now?

The following are some important tools to keep in your toolbox when you start dating.

Check with His References

A lot of times, the first stop for information is to be in touch with a guy's references. Typically, you should do this before you even agree to go on a date. If he's listed official references, give them a call. And if not, can you find a mutual acquaintance you could reach out to?

When you call up a reference, you want to ask open-ended questions like, "So, how would you describe his personality?" And then *let them answer*. Don't start "leading the witness" or giving them suggestions. Let them *talk*. You will learn more in their initial description of him than you will learn by asking questions.

As you go through this process, you want to find out what adjectives his friends use to describe him. Does it sound like he has a good reputation when you research him? Are people saying, "Oh, my gosh, he's the best! He's the one who always jumps in when we need help." Or does it sound like they're trying to avoid telling you the truth about him because the truth is not super flattering? Read between the lines and pay attention to what they're not saying.

What you find out may not be a reason to say no to a date. But it helps you fill in the picture of who he is, so you move forward with your eyes open. You should definitely ask about your deal-breakers and his goals and values, to establish whether it seems like it's good on paper.

If you don't have anyone to call, there's always Google. And of course, check out his social media, if he has any. Vetting the suggestions you get is a must.

Watch How He Relates to Others

The next way we learn about a guy is during the dating process.

The first thing to pay attention to is how he treats the people he's *not* trying to impress. He's trying to win you over, but his true colors may be revealed when he speaks to the waiter or the cashier.

That's why it's important to make sure we see the guy we're dating in different contexts, in different situations, and with different people. Depending on the world that you're dating in, this might mean meeting his family and friends. If he has bad character, it's going to seep out. How does he treat the waitress when she brings the wrong food? How does he react when he's cut off in traffic? Does he start cursing up a storm? How does he sound when he's talking to his mother on the phone? How does he speak about other people? Nastily? Or with appreciation and gratitude?

While we're dating, we want to have both eyes open for any red flags. So pay close attention here, because you could get a lot of important insights into what kind of guy he is. Target: a mensch.

Koso, Kiso, Ka'aso – *His Cup, His Pocket, His Anger*

The Talmud states that to really know someone well, you need to see him *b'koso*, *b'kiso*, and *b'ka'aso*. *B'koso* is in his cup – how he behaves when he's drunk. *B'kiso* is in his pocket – how a person relates to money. And *b'ka'aso* is in his anger – how he behaves when he's angry.

B'koso – in his cup. The saying goes, "When the alcohol goes in, the truth comes out." You see who someone really is when they've been drinking. Does he get nasty or crass when he has a few drinks? My husband gets happier and says more *divrei Torah* on Purim (the one holiday when it's sanctioned for Jews to drink heavily). Phew!

> **Handy Hebrew Helper:** *Divrei Torah* is the plural of *d'var Torah*, defined earlier. As a reminder, it means "words of Torah." A guy who talks about Torah or another positive subject when drunk…is probably safe.

B'kiso – **in his money.** This is subjective – meaning, it really depends on your personality. I know someone who is married to a man who is "careful with money," and it doesn't bother her, because she herself has very low material needs and really wanted someone responsible. On the other hand, if I were married to a guy like that, I would go insane! The fact is, how people choose to spend their money reflects what's really important to them. Does he spend a lot of money on books? On healthy food? On expensive liquor? On cars? On videogames and electronics? Does he give charity? Or does he only spend money on himself? What he spends his money on gives you an idea of what his values and priorities are.

B'ka'aso – **in his anger.** Okay, don't stage a fight so you can see how he is when he's angry! If you date long enough, it'll come up anyway. Or you can do research and ask his references if they have ever seen him angry.

"What did that look like?"

"Oh, he tends to punch the wall." (True story.)

Oh, really? Well, now you know. So, you could do some research, and then chances are while you're dating him, you will see him get irritated or stressed out or even angry at some point. Watch how he reacts and learn from it. Does he get angry often? Is he good at restraining himself? Does he try not to judge others? Or is he really a stickler about his point of view and not willing to see someone else's?

All the information that you gather here should then be used when you're looking at your deal-breaker list. If "able to compromise" is on your list and you find he is rigid and stubborn…well, then, it might be time to move on.

Consulting a Dating Mentor

So you're starting to get dates. And you're trying to be as smart as possible about getting information on the guy you're seeing.

But there is still one crucial piece about how to go through this in the smartest, best way possible. And that is to find a dating mentor.

In my experience, most people could benefit from a dating mentor. Across the board, for all ages, all religious stripes, it's so helpful to have someone in your corner who is truly objective. I always say to my clients that a dating coach is the only objective person in your life. I'm not your parent. "Just marry him! He has two legs! He's Jewish! Don't be so picky!" Like...really, Mom?

I'm not your single girlfriend, who is subconsciously thinking, "Oh, no! I'm going to have to go to those annoying singles events alone if she gets married!"

And I'm not the matchmaker, who is subconsciously biased because she's expecting a payout at the end. As a dating coach, I'm not biased, because my payment doesn't depend on the outcome. A dating mentor or coach just wants you to make good decisions for YOU.

Your mentor could be a married friend, an extended family member, a dating coach, a rabbi, a rebbetzin. The important thing is that whoever you choose as your mentor should be someone who has good advice to give about marriage and who understands what traits are important in a future spouse. So you want to speak to someone who has been happily married for, in my opinion, at least ten years. Because the first ten years is really just figuring out what marriage is about.

I know it's tempting to want to schmooze with your single friends about dating, but I wouldn't use a single friend as your go-to person or dating mentor. We want to go to people who have themselves successfully done what we're trying to do!

Basically, your mentor needs to know what marriage is about. Because when you know what marriage entails, you're going to date differently. You're going to prioritize different things. A dating mentor who has been happily married for ten years or more will be able to tell you what's important and what's not important to focus on when dating.

Now, try to choose *one* person as a mentor, and don't talk to too many different people. Because when you have too many cooks in the kitchen, it gets confusing. Having lots of voices in your head will just be a mess. Ideally, this should be someone who actually has the time available and whom you feel comfortable reaching out to. Because if you don't feel comfortable calling her, you're not going to!

Chapter 4

The Dating Process

Woohoo! You scored a date! You met a guy you're interested in, or someone saw your blurb and thought to set you up with someone interesting. However you got here, you are ready to start dating!

Now that you're about to jump in, we're going to talk about what to expect once we start going out (spoiler: it's *not* love at first sight!). Knowing what to expect here is so important because it helps us make sure that we're doing what we need to do and not walking away for the wrong reasons.

Despite what Disney might have taught us, most engagements don't happen overnight. So what should be the process from when we meet the guy to when we decide he's *the one*?

Or, in other words, what should be happening on the first date, second date, third date, and so on? What should you expect?

There are basically four stages of dating – the keep-it-light/should-we-spend-another-two-hours-together stage, the get-to-know-you stage, the emotional intimacy stage, and the leap-of-faith stage.[1] We're going to talk about all these stages and how we can optimize each one.

Stage 1: Keep It Light (Dates 1–2)

Important: the first date is not about asking yourself, "Is this my husband?" Please don't do that!

1   Rosie Einhorn and Sherry Zimmerman, *Dating Smart: Navigating the Path to Marriage* (New York: Menucha, 2013).

41

If at the end of the first date, you can say to yourself, "I wouldn't mind spending another two hours with this person," great, then go on a second date. That's really all you should be thinking about. Please don't get ahead of yourself, thinking: *Is this my husband? Does he check all the boxes on my deal-breakers list?* Just stay in the moment, be present in your body, and ask yourself at the end if you want to spend another two hours together. You can't possibly have enough info on date one or two to determine if he's your husband. Your vibe should be warm, receptive, smiley, friendly, interested, paying attention to what he's saying, and asking follow-up questions.

What to Talk About?

So what do you talk about on that first date? Really, the first date is just "airplane talk." If you were to get on an airplane and find yourself sitting next to a nice girl wearing a Jewish star, you'd start getting into a conversation with her, right? It's a short flight, like New York to Florida. It's only two hours. You're not getting into deep stuff like "What are your biggest fears and challenges?" That would be weird.

So we're dealing with questions like, "Where are you from? What do you do? What's your family like? Do you like your job? Did you ever go to Israel?"

And frankly, I'm a big fan of a two-hour coffee date for the first date, or something similar. I don't encourage dinner for the first date, because you could realize very quickly this person's not for you, and then you're stuck at dinner.

If you're working with a matchmaker, you could tell her you prefer a coffee date. And for religious girls, it's very typical to go out and sit in a hotel lobby or lounge and have a soda. If you're dating more freestyle, then you can suggest meeting for coffee when he asks what you want to do. We just want to see if we have a very basic connection – do we feel he's a nice, personable guy?

When in Doubt, Keep Going Out

Most of the time, we should give everyone a two-date minimum. Unless you're physically repulsed or he said or did something off-the-chart offensive: in that case, you don't have to go on a second date. But if you're unsure, speak to a mentor. You don't want to say no to someone too soon and regret it.

Why? Because everyone could have a bad day. Maybe his boss yelled at him today. Maybe he didn't get a good night's sleep, maybe he's feeling under the weather, maybe he's nervous. There are so many reasons a guy could not be a hundred percent his best self on the first date.

And this is true throughout your dating. If you're in doubt about something – you haven't figured out if he has the qualities you're looking for, or you're not sure you're comfortable with something – don't break it off, keep going out. It's always better to go on another date and get that clarity in your kishkes than to break it off and always be looking back over your shoulder, wondering if you ended things prematurely. My motto is: *No regrets.*

The Second Date Is More of the Same

What's your second date? Basically more of the same. It's still two to three hours. If you're working with a matchmaker, you can request that. If you're not working with a matchmaker, and he's taking you out at seven or eight o'clock, you could say, "You know, I have an early day at work tomorrow. I need to be home by ten thirty." Or, "So sorry, I had a really great time, I just have to get home, so I can have a good night's sleep."

Date two starts off with more airplane talk. I'm not opposed to getting deeper on date two, but let him lead that conversation if he chooses. Don't ask him, "So, what do you think are your biggest flaws?" Like, no…

Let Him Lead

I generally like the guy to lead the conversations. One of my clients said to me recently, "I'm nervous – what do we talk about on this date? What should I bring up?"

And I said, "Nothing. You just sit back and enjoy." Then after the date, this client said to me, "That was so much more relaxing than usual!" Basically, you should not be feeling this intense pressure to steer the date and think of conversations. That's really the guy's job. My opinion? Let him work for this a little bit!

Certainly, if there's a long silence and you feel like you want to bring something up, go for it. I'm not saying it's not allowed. But in general, the responsibility is on the man to lead the date, plan the date, organize the date, pay for the date, etc. And by the way, letting someone else take the lead does not come naturally to me! Just so you know: some of us have to work on it!

So now, by the end of the second date, you want to ask yourself again, would I like to spend another few hours with this person?

Stage 2: Getting to Know You (Dates 3+)

So we made it through the first two dates, and now we start to get a little more serious. From the third date on, we're in the real getting-to-know-you stage where we're thinking about our deal-breakers. Each date is a bit longer than those first two-hour dates. And from date three on, each date should have a purpose. You should not leave a date feeling you don't know him any better than you did before. That's a waste of a date.

We are focusing a bit more on attraction, asking ourselves if it is getting a little better each date and how we're feeling. Generally speaking, as long as it's getting a bit better over time, that's what we're looking for. Eyes and smile are where it's at for us. It's much easier to fix the outside than the inside. (Remember – it's easier to build muscles than *middos*!) So if there's anything in his physical presentation that's easy to fix – how he dresses, glasses, haircut, beard, teeth – please don't get stuck on it. Just tell yourself: *that's easily changeable*. Most guys (and gals) will want to present themselves in an attractive way for their spouse, so what you like will be important to him.

Each date, you should feel like you know this guy better and you have a better sense of how you feel about him. And he is getting to know you as well. It definitely shouldn't be only one person talking.

I really like the conversation-starting game Perfect Matches for the religious world or 36 Questions for others. These games are nice, because they keep you from being stuck on what to talk about next. You just pick out a card. It can make things a little more organic. I've also had clients who go through the game before a date and bring five cards that have questions that they want to know the answer to. If you play half a dozen cards per date, it's a very easy way to work on getting to know one another.

So each date should have a purpose, and you should definitely have your deal-breaker list in the front of your mind. If he's missing some basic stuff, that's the end. Obviously, best to talk it over with a mentor. But that's what the deal-breaker list is for, right? It's your GPS to finding Mr. Perfect-for-You. It also helps you know what questions you may want to ask on the next date – when there's a question mark next to one of your deal-breakers, you know you need more info on that one.

Early, transparent communication about goals and values will save you a lot of time and disappointment.

Two Dates per Week Minimum

Now, during this stage, I advise seeing each other at least twice per week. If either of you is not making time for two dates a week, you're not ready to get married. Press pause on your dating life. You'll revisit it in a few months when you're able to prioritize it.

If you want, after the first little bit of time, you could take it up to three dates a week. It's really up to you. Some women I work with get very overwhelmed when it's more than two dates a week. They feel like they don't have enough time to think and reflect and process, and they have a busy work life. And maybe they want more time to be working out and seeing their friends and doing other things. If you're like that, know yourself and keep it to twice a week.

For someone who feels it's harder to connect emotionally and get momentum, then I would up it to three times a week, because someone you see three times a week you're going to feel more connected to than someone you see only twice a week.

If a guy isn't even making time for one date a week, he is not marriage-minded. Or he's dating someone else. If you want to address this with him – not right away, but after a couple of weeks – you could say in a very warm and low-key way, "I know we're both super busy with work and everything else. I just think it's kind of hard to get momentum in the dating process when we're only seeing each other once a week. Can we both try to make more time for this?"

See what he says. You can add a Facetime or Zoom date if you need. Or he might be up for meeting in person. Or he might make it very clear to you that it's not worth your time to date him because he's not prioritizing his dating life right now.

No Marathon Dates

Now, here's a warning. No matter how often you see him in a week, no marathon dates! (In other words, don't let your dates go much longer than four or five hours.) Firstly, nothing good happens after midnight. And secondly, after about four or five hours, everyone runs out of things to say. I mean, I've been married over two decades, but if I'm out with my husband for many hours, we will run out of things to say at some point. That's not a red flag. But at some point, you may feel awkward. You think, *We ran out of things to say, maybe this isn't my husband.* No, no. It's because you were out for eight hours. It's just too long.

Level Up Your Contact

Also important is that 95 percent of your contact should be in person (rather than text or phone). And whenever he is in touch with you, you're always looking to level up your communication.

This means that first of all, texting should be reserved for "business" one-liners. *Hey, running five minutes late, be there soon.* Or, *Shabbat Shalom.* Or *Good morning. Good luck on your interview.* Those types of things.

If it's anything more than that, please don't text. Texting is rife with opportunities for miscommunication and misunderstanding, among other things. Instead, try to get him to a higher level of communication. For instance, you can say, *Hey, I'm not really able to text so much at work, but I'm available tonight at eight if you want to FaceTime.* Remember: phone is better than text, FaceTime is better than phone, in person is better than FaceTime. Our goal is to get our contact to the highest level that we can.

Stage 3: Developing Emotional Intimacy (Dates 5+)

After the first bunch of dates, when you know that he matches your deal-breaker list and your goals and values, the attraction is definitely on the chart and getting slowly better, and you have a nice time with him, you've established basic rapport. He's respectful to you, and you feel more or less comfortable. Now we progress to the next stage.

The third stage of the dating process I refer to as the "developing emotional intimacy" stage. This is where we move into really becoming vulnerable. I always say, I wish there was another way to date where you didn't have to be vulnerable. But there isn't. There is no way to decide whether this is your husband without it. For those of you who have been dating for a bit and have had some heartbreak, this can be difficult and scary. I know this from experience. But there's no alternative.

What happens in this stage is that we *slowly* begin to parcel out more personal information. We're not dumping it all on the table right away! But little by little, we should share stories that illustrate things we've struggled with or something we've learned about ourselves. And obviously, he needs to do the same so that it's mutual.

Now, when I say sharing past experiences, it doesn't mean you have to share everything. Do not dump all the skeletons out of the closet about previous relationships. Don't even talk about how long your relationships were. It is much more important to say something like, "Something I've learned over the years that I've been dating is that I really need someone who is *x*, *y*, or *z*." You want to talk about your deal-breaker list in the context of what you've learned about yourself through various experiences. But there's no need to get into specific memories.

The same is true for those of us who became more religious later in life. There's no need to dredge up past experiences. If you partied in college, he knows what that means. You don't have to give details. He's not dumb.

There will be some pieces of information that might be negative that you feel you have to share before you get engaged. I call these "bomb-drops." Some examples might be health issues, mental illness, medications that you're on, a learning disability, family dysfunction, abuse. These are things that need to be disclosed before you go under the chuppah.

When do we disclose these types of things? This is really hard to put numbers to, because it depends on the world you're dating in, but certainly not before date four. If you're in the more religious community, then bring it up on date five or six (or check with your rabbi). For others, once you know the chemistry is there, and you've checked off your deal-breakers and values, it's a good idea to share. If you're not sure when to bring this stuff up, consult your rabbi, coach, or mentor. Timing is important. You want to give him a chance to get to know you and like you before you dump everything on the table.

When you do bring it up, you want to discuss it in a very straightforward, low-key way. Kind of matter of fact, like, "I feel like we're at the point in our relationship where I should tell you that I have this or this condition," or, "I see a therapist for this," or whatever. "If you have any questions, I'm happy to answer them." But that's basically the gist of it. Sarah had Crohn's disease and disclosed this to the guys she dated once things were getting serious (per her rabbi's advice). Half a dozen boys broke up with her after hearing the news, which was very discouraging. However, her now-husband didn't view it as a deal-breaker, and he is everything she ever wanted in a man. We have to remember that if the person ends the relationship after hearing your news, then he isn't your soulmate.

Stage 4: The Leap of Faith (Engagement and Beyond)

The circles you are dating in will usually determine how long stage 3 lasts before you get engaged. So I can't give numbers for this. But the common theme is that you should date until you have full *clarity* that all the ingredients are there to have a successful marriage (see chapter 2), and not longer. We date to determine long-term compatibility, and that's it. Once you've determined that, there's no need to continue dating. Otherwise, it's kind of like the airplane that keeps circling the airport and doesn't land. We want to close the deal and land the plane, so we can move on with life.

Now we're up to stage 4, which I refer to as the leap of faith. Okay, I don't care if you're dating a month, six months, a year, ten years – there's that last 2 percent that involves walking off the cliff. This is true no matter how long you dated, no matter how much you know about him, no matter how many charts you filled out or how many conversations you had. Because you never really know how it is to be married to someone until you are actually married!

Many people get stuck here. Particularly men. Everything checks out. Intellectually, it makes sense. Yes, I'm attracted. Yes, we're emotionally connected. Check, check, check. You look forward to the dates. You miss him when you haven't seen him in a bunch of days. You feel there's mutual respect. You feel comfortable and safe with him. The common goals and values are there. But you still worry, *I don't know for sure…*

The truth is that taking this step is scary. And it's totally normal to be kind of afraid of it. Sometimes it's your own stuff (past trauma, broken home, lack of trust, and so on). Sometimes it's just that it's scary for everyone. And that's okay. It doesn't mean there's anything wrong.

However, if you're feeling a tremendous amount of anxiety as you approach engagement or once you're engaged, please be in touch with a mentor or therapist. It's possible that you're not confronting something important about the relationship, and you don't want to just go blindly forward with it and sweep everything under the rug.

Barring that kind of anxiety, though, it's good to know that the last step will be kind of scary no matter how perfect you are for each other, especially if you're not in your twenties anymore. So be ready for that.

And as you know, what comes after stage 4? Marriage! Hooray! We've made it!

Long-Distance Dating

We've covered the stages of dating. But before we can wrap up this chapter, there's one more thing we need to discuss. And that is long-distance dating.

Especially today with so much happening via Zoom and apps, chances are that many of you will do a bit of long-distance dating. And there are a few important things to know.

In a nutshell, long-distance dating is hard, because on a visit, you're seeing each other every day, and then you go back home and it's a big break. Really intense...and then nothing. This is honestly very dysfunctional and makes it difficult to have a normal relationship.

But when someone has been suggested to you who's not local, and he seems great, you definitely should not be limiting yourself based on geography. Just try to date smart.

Long-Distance Dating Hacks

- The dating process takes longer because it takes longer to get to know each other. Adjust your expectations accordingly!
- Start with two or three Zoom dates. Travel requires a lot of time and money – don't jump into it unless you think there's real potential!
- Remember: no marathon dating weekends! Even though it's tempting to spend time together nonstop on a visit, don't! This causes anxiety and can confuse and overwhelm you. Make sure you have some downtime to reflect and process the relationship.
- Between visits, keep up the Zoom/FaceTime dates (approximately an hour). Get dressed up, and make sure to see each other a few times a week so the momentum doesn't stall out.

Chapter 5

Dating with Dignity

O kay, ladies. Time to stop and assess. Because we could be doing everything that I wrote about in the previous chapters, and we could still be failing. Abysmally. And we need to understand why.

It's a Man's World out There

Let's begin by calling a spade a spade. It's a man's world out there. I know we're supposed to be liberated and all, and I'm not sure what happened. But things got pretty upside down and backwards.

Let me explain what I mean. You know the Jane Austen books/movies where the man courts the woman? Basically, he comes to her home while her family is there, plays some music for her, reads her some poetry, takes her for an afternoon drive in his carriage to look at the scenery… He says how beautiful she is, they discuss their values, and then maybe she lets him kiss her gloved hand and come back the next day and do the same thing all over again! After a number of these visits, he'll ask for her hand in marriage.

Who had the power in relationships back then? Was it the men, or the women? Well, the man had to please her! The dynamic was that a man courted a woman. She decided the parameters of the relationship and whether he was allowed to have the pleasure of her company tomorrow. And she owed him nothing in return.

Ever since the 1960s – the "Free Love" era – things have become a big mess. Now the man has the power. What are you, the woman, doing? You're texting him, you're messaging him on social media, you're asking him out. You're splitting the tab for the date. You're *friends with benefits*. You're *Netflix and chill*. You're giving him everything that a marriage entails even though you've got nothing on your finger. And then, after all that, he can dump you the next day and break your heart! Who has the power in this situation? I think the answer is clear. (Spoiler alert: it's not you.)

Secular Dating – Don't Waste Your Time!

In the secular world, you date primarily for fun, not to determine long-term marriage compatibility. You date for entertainment, you see movies (which by the way, is a terrible way to get to know a guy). You date to fool around, you date because it feels good. And then, six months, a year, three years later, you decide you want to figure out if you're compatible. And that's if he's even sticking around for that long.

When I meet with a new client for the first time, I do a dating history. I want to hear what's been going on over the last five, ten, fifteen, twenty years. Sometimes I'm writing *pages* of dating history – there are five years with this guy, eight years with this guy, three years with this guy, two years with this one. And I think, *Oh, my gosh, this is so much wasted time!*

But it's not just time, it's your heart! Each failed relationship into which you've invested your whole self only for it not to work out is like one more wall you're putting around your heart, making you more guarded and cynical the next time. *I'm not going to make that mistake again. I'm going to hold back.* You have your guard up.

That's how I felt before I met my husband. I had given up on finding Mr. Perfect-for-Me. I was totally cynical and jaded and distrustful.

So when I met my husband, I thought, *He seems nice. But, you know, that's not possible.* Because you start to feel like every guy is going to turn out to be a jerk. So the whole time, I was waiting for the other shoe to drop. Before every date, as I was putting on my makeup, I would say to myself, *Okay, just prepare yourself. This is the date when it's all going to blow up in your face, like it did every other time.*

How sad is this? I want to cry for myself! Obviously, it was a happy ending, because the shoe never dropped. But why did I have to feel like that? I had PTSD! I was traumatized. No one should have to go into marriage feeling that way.

But There's a Solution!

We appreciate the problem. Secular dating is just really bad for marriage. It's a man's world, and women start to think their whole job is to please the guy, and he never has to make a commitment. My favorite line is *Don't be a wife to a boyfriend.* It's time for us to take our feminine power back and stop giving it away. But how?

Fortunately, there is a way! And this concept is actually the reason I was first attracted to Torah Judaism. I didn't have any beautiful, lofty spiritual reason at first. God didn't come to me in a dream. I didn't even believe in God at the time! I was totally practical and pragmatic. Simply put, I was sick of the secular dating world. And I learned that Judaism offered a better solution. Period, full stop.

How do we date the Jewish way? It's pretty simple, really. The guy asks you out. He plans the date. He comes prepared with questions to get to know you. He pays for the date, and you owe him nothing in return, except the pleasure of your company.

Okay, let's quickly compare that to dating in the secular world. First of all, "dating" isn't even happening that much. It's more like…hooking up. A "situation-ship." Sometimes it might progress to actually going out on a real date (especially if you asked him out!). If the guy actually does take you out, there's this feeling, "Oh, you paid for my steak dinner. So I must owe you something." What kind of *something* do you owe him? Do I really need to say? But why should you owe him anything?

Shomer Negiyah – *Guarding Touch*

How does the Jewish way of dating avoid this problem? Well, in Jewish dating, we have a simple concept. It's called *shomer negiyah.*

> **Handy Hebrew Helper:** *Shomer* means guarding. *Negiyah* means touch. Guarding touch means being careful about how you use touch. In the religious world, *shomer negiyah* refers to men and women refraining from touching each other before they get married. For our purposes, guarding touch and not jumping into a physical relationship is just a smarter way to date.

If we're dating for marriage, we don't want to be wasting months or years of our lives with people who are not compatible with us or who are not serious. We've made our deal-breaker list. And now we want to date in a way that is conducive to determining compatibility. We want to be logical and smart and focused, and we want to weed out the guys who are not interested in us for the right reasons. And you know how we do that? *By taking the physical off the table.* If he's not getting any side benefits, and he's still asking you out, guess what? He really likes YOU.

Why Hands-Off Is the Way to Go

Let's stop for a minute and see why guarding touch, or being *shomer negiyah*, is such an amazing tool for finding the perfect match.

First of all, it's normal and healthy to want to connect physically with the opposite gender. That's how we're hard-wired.

But here's the thing. Touch is very powerful. Motivational expert Tony Robbins says that touch is one of the most powerful tools of persuasion.[1] Have you ever been shopping in a store where the salesperson is paid on commission? What does she do?

---

1   Team Tony, "The Power of Touch," Tony Robbins, https://www.tonyrobbins.com/mind-meaning/the-power-of-touch/.

She touches you. "Honey, can I help you find something?" (hand on your back). "Sweetie, come look at this" (steering you gently toward a clothing rack). And you're like, "Oh, thanks, I'd love to buy that overpriced dress!" Right?

Touch opens you up. It makes you more receptive. It makes you feel closer to the salesperson and more ready to buy something from her. Believe me, she wouldn't be doing it if it didn't work.

How does that play out on the dating scene?

The Power of Oxytocin

Discussion of the power of touch leads us to the discussion of the hormone oxytocin. Oxytocin is called "the bonding hormone" by psychologists because it makes us feel connected to people. Oxytocin is released into a woman's bloodstream when she gives birth and when she nurses her baby. And believe me, we need that oxytocin to become obsessed with a little mush that keeps us up at night and spits up all over us and just in general forces us to give of ourselves twenty-four seven. Oxytocin ensures that we keep taking care of our baby, even with all those sleepless nights!

The other time that God puts oxytocin into your bloodstream is when you're using affectionate touch. That includes touching family members, friends, and you guessed it – that guy you're dating. When you hug him, kiss him, cuddle – the more physicality, the more oxytocin is released. Add that to the "new love" hormones dopamine and serotonin, and now there's a cocktail of powerful hormones going through your body when you start a relationship. According to psychological studies, new love produces the same surge of dopamine that cocaine generates, causing extreme euphoria and a crash soon thereafter.[2] From the

---

2   Christian Nordqvist, "Falling in Love Hits the Brain like Cocaine Does," Medical News Today, October 27, 2010, https://www.medicalnewstoday.com/articles/205973#1.

minute you start touching Joe, you just feel so bonded to him! It's all the oxytocin and other hormones running through you.

But here's the thing: Is Joe worth bonding to?

The problem is that with all these infatuation feelings for him, you start to get kind of blurry on whether he's really compatible with you. Suddenly, all the clarity you got from making your deal-breaker list doesn't seem so clear anymore. *Like, I don't know, do you think being an axe murderer is a deal-breaker? I don't know. I feel like I could work with it! I'm into projects...*

We all know someone *else* this has happened to. Maybe a sister, a cousin, or a friend who was in a relationship with a guy who treated her badly or who didn't share her values. And you feel like saying, "What is wrong with you? Do you not see this? Don't you see how badly he's treating you?! Do you not see that you are totally incompatible? Why on earth are you staying in this relationship?"

I have one answer for you, ladies. Oxytocin. No, she does not see it. She's drunk on a love cocktail, completely blinded, her brain in a fog and not seeing him accurately.

Keep Your Head Screwed on Straight

So let me ask you, do you really want to go into a marriage having been blinded? Do you want to commit to someone for life after spending months without really paying attention to whether you're compatible?

We all know the answer is no! And that's why it's so important to hold off on the physical, so you can pay attention to every detail while you're dating.

You want to notice those red flags. How is he speaking to the cashier? How does he behave around his family and friends? Is he respectful to you? But when you're drugged up on oxytocin from the physical connection, you just won't notice. The "new love" chemical fog makes us feel like, *La la la. I'm so in love!*

Deal-breakers shmeal-breakers! This is so not good for us. Touch fogs the brain and clouds your judgment.

Would you ever buy a used car if you were drunk or high? Why not? Because you'd be much more likely to end up with a lemon! We don't want to date for marriage "drugged up" on love hormones. We don't want to be in the 60 percent divorce rate – we want to make the best decision we can.

Recently, a client of mine called me. I had spoken to Becca a year and a half ago just as she was starting to date someone. As she described the guy to me, I noticed some yellow flags. I told her to take the physical off the table (easier when you're always in public places) until she investigated these issues and gained clarity. And then I didn't hear from her for a year and a half (not everyone uses me properly). Well, Becca didn't take my advice. All the issues I was concerned about are still there. She's finally breaking up with him, but it's so much harder now that they've been physical and her heart is all intertwined. She wasted a year and a half of her life and is heartbroken, all because she made decisions about this relationship with her hormones instead of with her head.

Even without touching a guy, you will still be swayed by your feelings. You won't be completely objective. That's why it's so important to have a friend or a mentor or a coach (who wasn't drooling over how cute he looked on your last date) to talk things over with. But throw in physicality? Forget it. Your objectivity goes out the window!

Writer Michal Leibowitz summarizes the dilemma neatly in her op-ed "Dating Is Broken: Going Retro Could Fix It."[3] "Many of us go on dates seeking the spark of chemistry and tumble into bed, or relationships, often without determining whether our

---

3   Michal Leibowitz, "Dating Is Broken: Going Retro Could Fix It," *New York Times*, September 29, 2022, https://www.nytimes.com/2022/09/29/opinion/dating-courtship-relationships.html.

prospective partners pass the most basic of compatibility tests. It's almost as though we *want* to get hurt."

A study published by the American Psychological Association's *Journal of Family Psychology* found that couples who waited until marriage reported less consideration of divorce, higher relationship satisfaction, better communication, and superior sexual intimacy when compared with couples who jumped into a physical relationship within the first couple months of dating. "Rapid sexual initiation often creates poor partner selection because intense feelings of pleasure and attachment can be confused for true intimacy and lasting love," says Jason Carroll, one of the study's authors.[4]

But holding back on touch has another advantage – it keeps you from going crazy for a guy. We all know how women can get a little obsessed when the physical is part of the relationship. Suddenly we're stalking him, or parked outside his apartment… we get a little bit nuts.

But when you shelve the physical, it gives you control over your emotions. You're less *obsessed*. You're less desperate for him to call you back. Your thoughts run more like, *It's cool. Either we're compatible or not. I'd be sad if it ended. But I want to meet my husband. I don't want to waste time with someone who isn't serious.* Feeling more in command of yourself, almost a little more detached like this, is actually a really good thing when you're trying to decide if you want to marry someone.

Because of this, you also don't get as jaded when you have to break off relationships. With secular dating, after a while, you just don't want to do it anymore. You start to give up. But then, when you start dating *shomer*, you'll be shocked at how easily you'll be able to get over relationships. When a *shomer* relationship ends,

---

4   Jason S. Carroll, "Slow but Sure: Does the Timing of Sex during Dating Matter?" Institute for Family Studies, August 14, 2014, https://ifstudies. org/blog/slow-but-sure-does-the-timing-of-sex-during-dating-matter#:.

you can just say, "Not for me – next!" It's absolutely brilliant how the system *works*. Must be divine…

Dating *Shomer* Even When You're Not Religious

Obviously, if you're dating guys who understand what *shomer* means, you just say, "I date *shomer*," and you're done. *Hands off. Can't touch this.*

But a lot of women ask me, "What if I'm not religious? Can I still say, 'I date *shomer*'?" I say yes, absolutely. This is its own category. First of all, Judaism is not all or nothing. Don't feel like because you don't keep kosher or Shabbat that you can't date in the Jewish way.

Yet what if you're dating someone who has no idea what the word *shomer* means? How do you explain it?

Well, there's a little speech that you need to give him. And you're going to give it to him up front – as in, on the first or second date, early on. You don't want to wait until the end of the date, when he's already gearing up to give you a kiss and he leans in, and then you have to do "the dodge." Then it becomes awkward and uncomfortable. Find the right time to say it, but make sure it's early on.

So here is your script. You say something like this:

> I'm really enjoying getting to know you. And I'd really like to get to know you better. But I find that it's hard to get to know someone in a real and authentic way when the physical is part of the relationship. So, I'd like to take that off the table for now, and get to know each other in a real way. I hope you can respect that.

Do it in your own personality, your own words, whatever feels authentic. My trademark vibe is "feminine but assertive" – you're smiling and warm, but you're also holding your ground. You may encounter guys who end the relationship after you express your desire to date this way. That's okay – we don't want to be in a relationship or "situation-ship" with a guy who only wants to hook up. We only want to date someone who likes us for the right reasons and is marriage-minded.

Different Levels of Shomer

Now, ideally, you want to go cold turkey and break the touch addiction. But I know this is very hard. (And if you're already dating *shomer*, you can skip to the next section!) But let's say you're not ready to completely take the physical off the table. It doesn't have to be all or nothing. It's true that the ideal is calling off all physical contact until after the chuppah. If you're doing this, you're amazing – keep it up!

But if you find you can't manage that, you could at least try to wait as long as possible to do anything physical. This gives you a bubble of time where you are completely objective, and it enables you to eliminate the guys who aren't worth your time.

By the way, even secular dating coaches recommend this. Every dating book I've read advocates taking the physical off the table in the beginning stages of the relationship. Talk show host Steve Harvey has what he calls the "ninety-day rule."[5] He recommends that couples wait until they've been dating ninety days before being physically intimate. So if you can hold it together and be strong for the beginning stages, you will weed out the guys who are not marriage-minded or who just aren't that into you, as well as those who simply aren't compatible.

No matter what approach you decide to take, try to reserve *something* for marriage. So if you're totally secular and you're thinking, *Okay, I'm going to wait the first three months. But I can't imagine going to the chuppah without having done anything*, I'm

---

5   Steve Harvey, *Act Like a Lady, Think Like a Man: What Men Really Think about Love, Relationships, Intimacy, and Commitment* (New York: Amistad/HarperCollins, 2009).

not judging you. But protect yourself by not giving all of you until your man has made a commitment to your security by marrying you. Make it special in some way.

So you do you, but it's worth it to make the effort to resist the hormonal pull. The main thing is to have that bubble of objectivity in the beginning of a relationship. And trust me, you *will* thank me later.

Going Shomer: Client Close-Ups

Eliana's Story

Eliana was experimenting with being *shomer*, and she suggested to a guy that she wanted to wait for marriage. She gave her own version of the speech.

The guy said to her, "You know, being physical is a normal part of getting to know someone in a romantic relationship. So if you don't want to do that, I don't think we have a relationship."

She responded, "Cool. See ya!" And she left. Afterwards, she told me how happy she was. She realized at that moment that number one, he was not serious about her or about marriage. And number two, she had just saved herself months, if not years, of her life that she might have wasted with a guy who was not in it for the right reasons! She was so proud of herself for making the speech! His reaction revealed his true colors.

Alison's Story

Alison attended my dating class. Afterwards, she went home and was schmoozing with her brother. They were both secular. Alison told her brother, "I just went to a class, and the dating coach said I should make this speech when I'm dating." And she told her brother the speech.

Her brother said to her, "That would be so annoying if some girl I was dating said that to me."

So she said to him, "Would there be any situation where it wouldn't be annoying?"

And he said, "Duh – if I was seriously interested in her."

Case closed. From a man's mouth.

Jeremy and Sophie's Story

Jeremy and Sophie recently got married after dating for a while. Sophie wrote to tell me about their experience being *shomer* before they decided to get married. It was Jeremy's first time being in a *shomer* relationship. And at first, he was hesitant, but he said, "Um, okay, this is different, but I'll respect it."

Jeremy wasn't thrilled (and let's be honest, what Y chromosome on the planet is going to throw a party when his girlfriend says she's not going to touch him?), but he was willing to respect it and see how it went. Then what happened? He realized that he actually liked it better! Why? He said that you get to really know the person when you don't get the physical involved. A physical relationship tends to overshadow everything else, and it takes a much longer time to get to know the person.

Jeremy also articulated that he didn't want to break *shomer* because he wanted them to date with their brains. This would keep them from accidentally marrying the wrong person because they were being swayed by chemistry. He also liked the idea of not hurting her as much if it didn't work out.

They learned more about each other in a week of being *shomer* than a guy she had dated for two and a half years, because all they were doing was talking. Of course, then they got married and could bring the physical in. But even *he* was impressed by how it changed the relationship while they were dating!

Mike and Erica's Story

Mike and Erica – both completely secular – dated all through college. They had a full-on relationship with everything that entails for four years. Then Erica went to a Jewish outreach program on her college campus and heard about *shomer negi-yah*. The next time she saw Mike, she told him what she had learned about. And she said, "I think we should try it."

Again, Mike didn't throw a party, but he really cared for her. So he said, "Okay, we could try it." They were engaged within six months and married another six months after that. And Mike has told me to my face, "I'm not sure we would be married, had she not done that." It just gave them the clarity they needed to know that they really loved each other and wanted to commit. Being *shomer* "landed the plane."

Stay Safe: Avoid Being Alone

Now, I know everyone may choose to hold off on the physical in different ways. But the biggest practical pointer to be able to do things right is to keep the laws of *yichud*. *Yichud* means "seclusion." Jewish law forbids men and women being secluded with one another when they are not married.

Handy Hebrew Helper: *Yichud* is the Hebrew word for seclusion. The laws of *yichud* teach that a man and woman who are neither married to each other nor first-degree relatives (grandparent, parent, sibling, child)

The analogy I give is this: If you were a diabetic, would it be smart to work in a candy store? No. If you're attracted to each other, it's for sure gonna be difficult to keep hands off! That's healthy and normal! Instead, you want to set yourself up for technical success. So if you're really attracted to a guy, but you know you need to give things time to figure out if he's marriage material and compatible with you, would it be smart to go back to his apartment? Not smart. It's him and his body and your body may not be secluded together in a space that can't be easily accessed by others. For our purposes, *yichud* means *don't go up to his apartment and don't have him up to yours!*

against your better judgment. That's three to one: you lose.

That's why we're going to avoid being secluded. You're always around people. You don't go to his place, he doesn't come to your place. You're at a restaurant, at a lounge, getting a coffee, going for dessert, playing mini golf, walking through the park during the day. You're not closing any doors where no one can walk in. 'Cause by the way, if he says he wants to come up and "see your apartment" or "watch a movie" – translation: he wants to hook up.

Now, I hate to do this, but in case you're not taking this seriously, I'm gonna dredge up horror stories from my clients. A girl I know was dating in the religious world. And just because someone looks religious doesn't mean that Judaism has permeated his heart. So she stupidly allowed him up to her apartment on the second date, and he forced himself on her. She ended up getting pregnant. This is a religious girl I'm talking about. She had to have an abortion, and it was an extremely traumatic experience all around.

I had another client who was driving with a guy at probably three in the morning (which I really don't advise – I repeat, nothing good happens after midnight!). Anyway, he pulled the car over in a deserted area and tried to do something against her will. Thank God she knew some form of martial arts, and she escaped. And she had been dating him for three months! She thought she knew him!

If you don't want to keep *shomer negiyah* or be careful of *yichud* for the reasons I've given – which are pretty intelligent and meaningful reasons – at the very least, do it for your own safety. Never be secluded with a man in a place where someone cannot easily find you.

But Don't We Need a Test Drive?

You've seen that there is a solution to the problem of secular dating. And you've seen that the solution involves holding off on physical contact so you can keep your head screwed on straight and really get to know a guy. But a lot of people are still a little skeptical.

They ask me, "How can you decide to marry someone if you haven't like…tried things out with him first?" Like you test drive a car before you buy it! How can you decide to marry someone without seeing whether you're compatible physically?

This is a normal question. Of course, religious Jews have been getting married this way for centuries and seem to be doing fine, but it is kind of scary to think of discovering your physical relationship only after the wedding.

The thing is, this question comes from looking at sexuality in a very secular way. See, in the secular world, it's basically a skill. Right? You've probably seen the headlines on Cosmo: "Five tricks to drive him crazy." It's like being good at tennis.

But in Judaism, intimacy is not a skill. It's a physical expression of the emotional, spiritual, and psychological relationship that you share with this person. So if you're married, and you love him, and he loves you, and you're spiritually connected, and you're emotionally connected, and he's there for you, and he's a good listener, and he's a kind person, and you're connected in every way, do you think it's going to be bad physically? It's not likely. Yes, there's a small percentage of the population where there will be dysfunction. (And there are solutions for that.) But the average couple who love each other and who are connecting in these deep ways use the physical as an expression of that love. Bottom line: technique can be learned; character can't.

Physical intimacy is not supposed to be a skill that can be used on different people. It's supposed to be reserved for the one person you share your life with. And if you test drive all your relationships, it loses that special quality.

By the way, research supports this.[6] Getting married *without* test-driving is actually good for the longevity of your relationship. There's research that shows that being intimate before marriage does not necessarily "test the quality of the relationship" and guarantee a better chance of success. Actually, the opposite: women who were intimate before marriage were 15 percent more likely to get divorced! And early marriages in which neither partner had ever been intimate before have some of the lowest divorce rates around. So the test-drive-before-you-buy theory really doesn't work.

The other thing about not touching before marriage – and I think we can all agree on this – is that you know if you are attracted to someone without touching him. You're either thinking, "Ewww!" or "Oh, my gosh! He's adorable!" It might take a little time for the attraction to build up, but if it's the right person for you, you do not have to touch even his pinkie to know that you are super attracted to him. And then, of course, everything else will fall into place.

Kimberly's Story

Kimberly (who had never dated *shomer* before) met, dated, and married her husband during Covid. She told me it was like "forced *shomer*" because they were afraid to get close or kiss, so they dated in the Jewish way by default. She said it was amazing, because very quickly they were able to see that they were compatible, had chemistry, and were committed. In short, it helped "land the plane."

---

6   Brad Wilcox and Lyman Stone, "Too Risky to Wed in Your 20s? Not if You Avoid Cohabiting First," *Wall Street Journal*, February 5, 2022, https://www.wsj.com/articles/too-risky-to-wed-in-your-20s-not-if-you -avoid-cohabiting-first-11644037261.

It Only Takes One

People are often a little skeptical about the idea of dating with dignity at first. *Shomer negiyah* is different from what you're used to, and it's difficult! And it's especially hard if it seems like the guys aren't going for it. What if you're losing one guy after another because they're not willing to try it out?

But what this is really about is knowing that you're worth it. You're a high value woman. That's your vibe. If you want to date me, you're gonna have to work for it. You can't respect my boundaries? Goodbye.

And if most of the guys walk, that's actually a *good* thing. That's the whole point – because all you need is that one mensch. And you don't *want* to keep wasting time with anyone else. Don't settle for less than you deserve.

Unhealed wounds (from childhood or past relationships) create a lot of desperation. When we don't have good self-esteem, we settle for "breadcrumbs" that resemble love but aren't the real thing.

Dating with dignity is what attracts the guy who will *treat* you with dignity. And isn't that what we want from the guy we plan to marry?

Chapter 6

Image Integrity

I magine the wardrobe you would put on if you were inter-viewing for a C-suite position at a big company. Now imagine what you might wear if you were interviewing for a barista job at a local pub. Maybe a little different, right?

Now imagine you went on the interview for the C-suite job dressed like you were interviewing to be the barista. Good idea? Probably not.

As frustrating as it might be, research has shown again and again that appearances count. Some styles of dress command more authority and respect. Other kinds, less so.

Body language expert Joe Navarro says, "It's interesting how we profess to dismiss matters of appearance, considering how obsessively we focus on looks.... Our...fixation makes sense, though, when you understand appearance as a form of nonverbal communication."[1] In other words, how we look is a way that we communicate to other people.

So if that's the case, what about when it comes to dating? Is there an equivalent to dressing like you're interviewing to be the barista, when you're really qualified to be the CEO?

Absolutely. Many of us dress like we're interviewing to be the girlfriend. Sexy, cute, fun. Easy to hire and *easy to let go*. But if

---

1   Joe Navarro, *Louder Than Words: Take Your Career from Average to Exceptional with the Hidden Power of Nonverbal Intelligence* (New York: HarperCollins, 2010), 7.

we're interviewing for the wife position, maybe we need to present ourselves differently?

Make the Outside Match the Inside

In order to find our soulmate, we have to date with our soul. We have to start thinking about what message we're sending with the way that we dress and behave. Yes, you are communicating a message! What do you want to highlight? Your character traits, your personality, your brain, your soul? Or the abs that you worked out at the gym and your other physical assets? Are you communicating that you're desperate for a guy's attention? That you have a great body to offer? That you're interested only in a fling?

Or do you want to send the message that there is so much more to you than meets the eye – *you're going to have to look deeper if you want to get to know me.* You want your vibe to be *I'm not desperate for guys' attention; I'm cool and confident because I know I'm going to find the one special guy for me, who's going to value me for my inner self.*

I sometimes bring a stylist into my dating classes to give advice to people about putting themselves together. She calls it "image integrity." Image integrity, which is connected to the Jewish concept of *tzniut*, basically means that your outside presentation should match your internal message.

This applies in every context. It's especially easy to visualize when you think of going to a job interview or going into politics. You wouldn't show up for an interview for an office job wearing a micro-mini and a tank top, right? Because it would be the sending the wrong message. And you wouldn't show up for a presidential debate wearing a bikini! Everyone knows that these

> **Handy Hebrew Helper:** *Tzniut* is a Hebrew word that is sometimes translated as *modesty* or *dignity.* For religious Jews, it describes a specific mode of dress and behavior that is incumbent on

men and wom-en to maintain a degree of privacy around the physical and highlight the spiritual aspects of a person. For our purposes, *tzniut* is about presenting ourselves in a way that is consistent with our goals. We want a serious guy who respects us for who we are inside? Then we have to dress the part of the woman who knows that she is more than just her body.

ways of dressing make people focus on your body and not on your essence.

But why is it that when we date, suddenly we're all about showing off our sexuality instead of our soul? Really, when we date for marriage, it should be kind of the same as when we're looking for a job. Put-together, classy, pretty, dignified, expressing who you are inside, and not overly sexy.

A Tasteful Frame for a Fabulous Picture

Imagine a really beautiful, expensive Monet painting. But now I put it into a huge frame with a twelve-inch molding of bling and glitter and sequins. Are you going to notice the beautiful painting of water lilies in the middle of the wall? Or are you going to notice the flashy, dis-tracting frame?

That's what dressing in a super-attention-seeking way does to us. It distracts people so they notice what we look like, but they don't notice who we are. This is not what we want.

We want to be presenting ourselves on dates in a way that highlights our inner qualities.

Now, by the way, this did not come naturally to me at all. When I first started becoming more connected to Judaism, my friend and I were going to synagogue, and I didn't have even one item of clothing in my entire closet that was okay according to Jewish law! Everything was like…teensy. This was a slow process for me. I'm *so* not judging anyone.

But the truth is, you don't have to be a religious Jew to realize that image integrity just makes sense. Look up advice on how to dress for the holiday office party and you'll find that displaying a lot of skin is a professional faux-pas. "Remember the purpose of the event," says *Business Connect Magazine*.[2] This advice translates very well into dating. Low-cut, tight, sheer, and otherwise revealing clothing puts all the focus on your body and not on your essence as a human being. Just as overly revealing clothing may interfere with the goal of business networking at the office party, it can also interfere with your goal of determining compatibility for marriage on a date.

I have a friend who was a buyer for a luxury clothing store before she became religious, and she used to help people shop. She said two things. Number one, if the curve under your chest or your backside is visible to the general public, the outfit is too tight. This was from a woman who was helping secular women dress in a way that was pretty and flattering!

The second thing she said is that at an upscale retailer, there's more fabric in women's clothing. When you shop at a fast fashion chain, the clothes may be so tiny you wonder if they're for a person or a doll. Ninety-nine percent of the stuff there is tacky. It's interesting that as you go up in price in women's clothing, things become more covered and more modest. Think classy. You don't need to shop at high-end stores to find modest items, but look for classic, well-made clothing, and don't choose outfits that leave nothing to the imagination.

Achieve Image Integrity

At some point in my Jewish journey, I was asking myself, *Why am I always meeting these players? Why can't I meet a nice, marriage-minded guy?* And then I realized that the message I was sending – not just with how I dressed, but how I spoke, how I walked,

---

2   "Attending a Corporate Event? Check Out the Dress Codes, Do's & Don'ts, and What to Wear," *Business Connect Magazine*, March 13, 2023, https://www.linkedin.com/pulse/attending-corporate-event-check-out-dress-codes/.

my whole vibe – was not oriented toward attracting a guy who was serious about marriage.

My soul was crying out, *I just want to get married to a nice guy*, but then everything else was sending the opposite message! It was no wonder the guys were confused. Guys who were marriage-minded were thinking, "Oh, she doesn't look like she's serious, marriage-minded material." And guys who were not interested in marriage were thinking, "Oh, she looks like she's interested in a good time." I really wanted something serious, but my whole messaging was not in congruence with how I felt.

Move toward Modesty

So even if this is not your favorite thing (especially in the summer!), and even if in your regular life, you don't want to take on the Jewish way of dress, I urge you to dress a little bit closer to the modesty model on your dates. I know everyone reading this book wants to meet a guy who is interested in your soul, who falls in love with who you are inside.

When we overemphasize the physical part of ourselves, when we're advertising our sexuality – both by the way we dress *and* the way we behave – it's harder for a man to focus on our inner self. So no matter how you dress the rest of the time, try to be a little bit more covered on your dates. Try not to wear things that are super tight and advertising everything. Same with low-cut, sheer, or super short. Just err on the side of keeping things a little more conservative.

This goes back to the picture frame. Our body is the picture frame. And our soul is the beautiful Monet painting. You want the guys you're dating – and especially the guy you marry – to focus on your soul, on who you *are*. You don't want him getting so distracted by the flashy outside that he can't see what's inside the frame.

Still Be Put Together

On the other hand, I can't put the picture up on a wall without a frame. And if this is really a Monet, I can't put a dinky little plastic frame around it. That doesn't go together.

A framing expert would tell you that a picture frame is meant to highlight the painting and draw your eye into it, not distract from the painting itself. Similarly, how you present yourself on the outside should still be pretty and put together. It should be dignified and classy and complement the picture.

There are women who have a hard time with presenting a good first impression. Some women even think it's not important at all and don't want to be bothered about how they look. They say, "He should just like me for who I am regardless." But just as we don't want to take away from what's inside by putting too much attention on the outside, we also don't want to take away from what's inside by using an unattractive frame.

If you're not sure how to put yourself together, speak to someone who can help. Maybe it's a friend or family member with a good fashion sense. Or watch some handy YouTube videos. Sometimes looking nice is just about wearing different colors or a belt or scarf or pretty jewelry, doing your hair, throwing on a little different makeup, whatever. Basically, do what it takes to be pretty and put together. You'll be glad you did.

Use Makeup as a Tool

One of my clients, Rita, was dating a guy. One day, she was at the beach with no makeup on, and he just showed up. Rita was embarrassed and said, "Sorry I don't have any makeup on." And he told her, "Great. I didn't want to date Sephora. I want to date you." I thought that was the cutest thing ever.

When it comes to using makeup, we're not trying to be Sephora. We just want to use it to highlight our own natural beauty (and maybe conceal things that we want to camouflage a little bit).

Obviously, once you're married, he's going to see you without makeup. We all know that. But while we're dating, we still need to put our best foot forward.

Get a Feel for Modesty

If you're reading this and thinking, *Oh, my gosh, I wouldn't know the first thing about how to dress modestly*, do not fear. You can speak to a stylist about it or contact me. This is one of my areas of expertise. If you are interested in tips on how to put outfits together that are modest but still cute, this is something I've worked on for over twenty years. And I buy much of my clothing in normal stores, online and at the mall, although there has been an explosion of modest fashion brands, which is fabulous! If you just search online for long-sleeve or three-quarter-sleeve midi, you have gajillions of cute dresses and skirts and outfits available.

To go over some basics – here are some examples of ways to dress with image integrity:

- Higher neckline, instead of plunging V
- Short or long sleeves, instead of sleeveless
- A-line or tailored, instead of bodycon
- Midi length, instead of micro-mini
- Elegant heels instead of five-inch stilettos

Review Online Profiles and Photos

Now, everything that we're talking about with image integrity applies to your online image as well. Which means that first of all, if you're on social media, please look at your profile from an outsider's perspective. Pretend you're a guy that you just met. And he's researching you online, which is the first thing they all do. Take a look at your profile on social media through his eyes.

You may want to get rid of some of the pictures or change what's easily viewable. You learn a lot from someone's social media profile. When I'm researching a guy, what if I see tons of pictures of him arm and arm with scantily clad women? Or maybe all of his posts are virulent political stuff? On the other hand, maybe he's posting pro-Israel stuff or sharing adorable animal videos.

Basically, you can learn a lot about someone from their social media profiles. But when it comes to *you*, make sure that he's getting the message from you in your online presence that you want to send. Are you giving out the party girl vibe? Or do you look like someone he's going to take seriously and date for marriage? This is different for everyone, but if you have any doubts, comb through your profile and see if there's anything you want to clean up.

A quick note on pictures. I have mixed feelings regarding pictures on dating resumes and sites. Obviously, a picture cannot capture a soul. But in our world today, they are often requested or expected. So if you're going to send or post pictures for dating purposes, I'm generally in favor of either getting them professionally done or getting a friend who is good with a camera to take them. I don't mean a whole thing where you're touched up and all that stuff. But just something that looks professional. It shouldn't be your selfie from your iPhone with poor lighting and your friends next to you.

It's not a bad idea to take a picture from a *simchah*. This could be your brother's bar mitzvah or someone's wedding, and you're wearing something pretty and you have your hair and makeup done. Then you can have someone who knows what they're doing take a picture, or even have the photographer take a picture and send it to you. Use that for any online dating profiles or *shidduch* resumes.

Handy Hebrew Helper: *Simchah* means happiness, and it also refers to life cycle events, such as a bris, bar mitzvah, or wedding. For our

So that's that for image integrity. Think of yourself as going on an purposes, professional or even amateur photos from a *simchah* can be really nice to send to a prospective date.

interview for a serious position: wife! And use your clothing, body language, and behavior to let guys know that you are marriage-minded and looking for a guy who is ready to honor and cherish you.

Chapter 7

Devorah's Dating Don'ts

Up until now, we've pretty much covered the basics: deal-breakers, the ingredients of a good marriage, the dating process. And we've talked about the importance of holding off on the physical and making sure we are sending the right messages with our dress and behavior.

Now I want to talk about some of the most common mistakes I see young women making in dating. I call these "Devorah's Dating Don'ts," the common pitfalls and bad patterns in dating, and it is *so* important to avoid these when we're dating.

Breaking up with Mr. Pareve

Who's Mr. Pareve? It's the guy you go on two or three dates with, and there's no real reason to say no. You're not grossed out by him. He didn't say anything offensive. He basically has what you're looking for on paper, or at least so far. He seems like he's in your ballpark. But he's just...*pareve*. Nothing amazing, right?

Handy Hebrew Helper: *Pareve* is the status of a food that is neither milk nor meat (such as veggies). It's neutral. For our purposes, *pareve* is the guy we're kind of neutral about. There's

Don't break it off with Mr. Pareve after only a few dates!

Instead, please keep dating him. I'm begging you. The thing with Mr. Pareve is that if you date him long enough, he'll either become Mr. Yay or Mr. Ewww eventually. You just have to give it time.

nothing *wrong* with him, but we're not super excited about him either.

So don't break up with someone just because the attraction hasn't yet clicked into place. Many, many of my clients ended up marrying guys who started off as Mr. Pareve. And by the time they got engaged, they were *excited* to marry him and attracted to him! We're not talking about Mr. Ewww here – I would never tell you to go on a second date with someone who grosses you out.

And if you're wondering how you can get yourself to feel more attracted, one thing to remember is that for women, physical attraction comes largely from emotional connection. So if you're having deeper conversations, and you're connecting in a deeper, more emotional way, the physical attraction will often follow.

When my clients are struggling with dating Mr. Pareve, I suggest they examine their dates for any moments when they did feel more drawn to him. Then, whatever they were doing in those moments – copy and paste! Do more of that! If it was seeing him in a more casual environment, then have a casual date. Go play mini golf. Or if you think he's cute when he gets dressed up and you go out to dinner, do that. If it's during a DMC (deep, meaningful convo) that you felt more connected, do more deep schmoozing! Make sure you have given Mr. Pareve a very serious shot before you even think about saying no.

We never want to live with regrets, looking back, thinking perhaps we ended things prematurely. Remember, it's always better to give it an extra date (or two) to get that elusive clarity in our kishkes. Obviously, if you've given it a good amount of time and done the things I'm suggesting and you're just stuck feeling pareve, it's probably time to end it. But just to be sure, it's good to consult with a mentor. Because with a little patience, Mr. Pareve might just turn out to be Mr. Perfect-for-You!

Expecting Opposite Traits in the Same Person

This was one of my mother's most important pieces of dating advice. She said to me, "If you are drawn to a particular trait, then you can't complain about the negative expression of that same trait."

Every positive has a flip side: Chana Levitan terms it "the challenge of the gift."[1] So let's say you are Miss Go-Getter who's a super Type A personality. And not surprisingly, since we usually marry the guy who complements our strengths and weaknesses, you end up marrying Mr. Chill.

He's super youthful, laid back, spontaneous – a fun guy. Now, you married him because you like those qualities, and they complement you. But being Mr. Chill has its flip side also, right? He may not be much of a go-getter, he may not be as responsible or make as much money, and so on.

A lot of people, when they discover the flip side to their spouses' traits, begin to complain about them.

Here's the problem: you can't expect to have a person with only the positive sides of a particular trait. That doesn't exist! So you need to decide for yourself, what's more important? Having a guy who's really responsible with money, for example, or having a guy who's willing to spend lavishly on you? Or could you come more to the middle on both of those opposing traits?

But you're not going to find two opposites in the same person. If he's a chilled-out guy, he may forget to pay the credit card bill on time. If he's an intense guy, he may be kind of rigid and have a hard time being spontaneous. Likewise, if he's really responsible with money, he might not get you as many gifts or spend as freely. But if he's the type to spend freely, saving up for that vacation or house might not be in the books or might create a lot of debt.

---

1   Chana Levitan, *That's Why I Married You! How to Dance with Personality Differences* (Jerusalem: Gefen Publishing House, 2016), 16.

If you like the positive side, and that's what's really important to you, then it becomes your job in dating (and in marriage) to overlook the negative side and remind yourself that the same thing that makes him frustrating in one way makes him the perfect guy for you in other ways.

Confusing Bad Habits with Bad Character

It's easier to build habits (which can improve with coaching) than character traits (which are hard to change). We might meet a guy who actually has really good character and a really good heart, but has some bad habits. It's important to learn how to distinguish between these two so we don't end up throwing out the good guy just because of some personality quirks. Sometimes, it can be tricky.

Melissa's Story

I was coaching Melissa. After a third date, she said to me, "I'm breaking up with this guy."

I asked why.

Melissa said, "Well, he talks about himself a lot. He interrupts me. And he doesn't ask me questions about myself. So clearly, he's selfish and egotistical, and I'm breaking up with him."

I suggested, "Well, a bad habit can present similarly to a bad character. Like, maybe he just needs a wife to tell him that he's interrupting? Maybe you're right, and he's a really egotistical guy. Or it could be that he just has a bad habit."

I said to her, "You have nothing to lose by going on a fourth date and bringing it up."

Whenever we bring something up, we're being feminine but assertive. We have a smile on our face; we say it nicely. And I told her to say, "I'm sure you didn't realize, but you were kind of interrupting me a lot. And it's sort of hard to get to know someone when, like, only one person is talking."

So she practiced this little script. And I told her, if he has bad character, what's he going to respond? "You're nagging me already on the fourth date?!" He'd be totally defensive, gaslighting, not taking responsibility for anything. Goodbye! We achieved our goal – total clarity.

But if he has good character, and it's just a bad habit, what's he going to say? "Oh, my gosh, that's terrible. I was interrupting you? I didn't realize! I'm so sorry. Of course I want to get to know you. Please remind me if I ever do that again!"

Well, when she got back from the date, she said, "How did you know exactly what he was going to say?"

Thank God, they're happily married. Good guy, bad habit.

This story makes me so happy because this couple were both in their mid-forties and never married, and she would have missed out on this person who is her soulmate because she misread the signs and assumed he was a bad person. Really, he had a good core – he was just rough around the edges and needed to refine his habits a little bit.

Now, if it is a bad habit that the guy has, then it is not a deal-breaker. But it's also important to know what to expect. When you were biting your nails as a kid, and your mom told you to stop, it wasn't the next day you stopped biting your nails forever. It takes time to break a bad habit. You needed reminders. So if you discover a bad habit, it's not going to disappear overnight. No worries if you have to remind him a few times. As long as you see him making a sincere effort – and real progress – that's enough.

In general, when it comes to these things, I like the idea of red flags versus yellow flags. A red flag is something off the chart that is indicative of bad character or abusive or controlling tendencies. Immediate deal-breaker.

But a yellow flag is where you see something negative in his behavior or speech and you're not sure – like a guy who interrupts.

Whenever you see a yellow flag, you want to put your antenna up and look for more info. Gather more data. Pay attention to it going forward. Is it just a bad habit, something you can talk to him about and he can work on? Or is it a sign of something deeper?

Some women will break up at this point, but that could mean they're missing out on the guy for them! So we want to hold off on judging until we have a chance to know more. Everyone has some bad habits. If we hold out for the guy who doesn't have any, we will literally be waiting to get married *forever*.

Being Drawn to the "Bad Boy"

Let's talk for a minute about the bad boy. You know the kind I'm talking about: he's cool, he's smooth, he's suave, he's got every line perfectly curated, he's a player.

For some reason, women are often addicted to this type. My theory is that many women are drawn to very masculine men, and sometimes, it can seem like this bad boy package is super masculine, when it's really not.

Ladies, by the way, do you know why every line he says sounds so smooth? Because he's been practicing on tons of girls before you, and he will continue to hone his skills on many girls after you...

This was what happened with my first client ever, Elizabeth. She had just started dating her now husband. And she said to me, "I don't know if I like him. He's just so...nice." As if that's a bad thing!

I took her dating history, and she had dated one player after the next. One guy cheated on her. The other guy was emotionally abusive. And on and on.

I asked her, "Did you have a lot of chemistry with those guys who treated you badly?"

Of course, the answer was yes. So much chemistry! These guys knew how to talk to her. They knew how to make her feel amazing. "But," I pointed out, "where did that get you?" Oh, right. Cheated on and brokenhearted.

So now, Elizabeth was dating her husband-to-be and she happened to run into one of these bad-boy exes, and she started doubting this nice guy because she was attracted to the bad boy! Even though she *knew* what a jerk he was…she was thinking, *No, no, I'll be the one to convert him!*

Stop. You're not going to convert him! Thinking you can drastically change someone is a dangerous game.

I said to her, "You're thinking about Mr. Player or Mr. Swag in a positive way. Like it's so great with guys like that. And you felt so much chemistry. And dating them is so exciting. And he says all the right things."

I suggested, "Instead, I want you to picture a label on his head that says 'cyanide.'"

What if I said to you, here's a glass of water – there's a 1 percent chance that there's a lethal dose of cyanide in here. Would you drink it? No, right? These guys – there's like a 99 percent chance that they are poison. It will not end well! So you have to visualize "cyanide" on his forehead. And tell yourself, *I don't want to date poison. I know I'm going to get hurt.*

You can actually break our addiction to the bad boy this way. You just need to remind yourself where it got you and where it will get you again.

I know, I know, when he looks at you, you feel like you're the only woman on the planet…until two seconds later when he's looking at someone else. What do we want instead? We want a mensch who's smitten with us! Just recite that in your head.

If you find that you're attracted to these types who are not really treating you with respect, my guess is that working on self-love might be a good option (see chapter 1). Because apparently, there's a part of you that feels you don't deserve a really good guy who's going to treat you well. You're always attracted to that rush of adrenaline from the guy who's maybe going to call, but he might not. Here's where you need to know your worth – you're a high-value woman, and you deserve someone who will treat you right. When you love and respect yourself and you remember that you deserve a mensch, a guy who really cherishes you, this kind of behavior stops being so appealing. You'll start to think, *Maybe be a bit reliable? Maybe stop looking at other women when you're out with me?* When you start noticing these behaviors, you won't even have to work so hard to break the bad-boy addiction!

It's a little bit like eating junk food and candy versus a healthy, satisfying meal. The junk food is sooo yummy and alluring, and the sugar high is intoxicating – but it immediately leaves us with a sugar crash and feeling gross. When we say no to the short-term gratification of the junk food, we end up being much more satisfied by the healthy food in the long run. The "bad boy" will give you a sugar rush, but he'll also leave you feeling gross and empty. The mensch is like a great, healthy meal – leaving you feeling content and stable.

Also, keep in mind that it's not an either/or binary choice. Women often think they need to choose between the vanilla/boring guy who's marriage material versus the "bad boy" with whom you have crazy chemistry. Safe versus sexy. But there's an option 3 – the good guy who's committed, to whom you become more and more attracted over time.

Dating Guys Who Aren't Marriage-Minded

This kind of goes with what we said about the bad boy, but it's a little different. The point here is that you have to believe a guy if he tells you he's not interested in marriage right now. Believe it or not, guys are much more honest than we are.

So, if a guy says, "I just want to let you know that I'm not really in the place right now to have a serious relationship," don't get starry-eyed and start thinking that you will convince him. Listen to what he's saying! He's being honest, okay? Some of us gravitate toward unavailable men due to wounds from childhood (another reason therapy is a great idea); we want to break this bad habit.

In general, don't take on "a project." Don't think that you're going to reform the lifelong player into a marriage-minded suburban husband. This is just not going to happen.

The truth is that you can't marry someone and have a to-do list for their self-improvement. I mean, of course he's going to change over time, and so will you. But he might not change in the exact ways that you want him to. Which is why you have to be able to say under the chuppah that even if he never changed, you would still be happy. He's a fantastic guy. He matches my deal-breaker list, we're on the same page. He makes me laugh. We have fun together. Maybe some of these things that I don't love will change, but I'm not holding my breath. I accept him for who he is.

Now, if a guy isn't marriage-minded, that is a deal-breaker. Because you're not going to convince him to want to get married… The only way to really know if he is a marriage-minded person, aside from having him tell you that he isn't, is to take all the side benefits off the table. Meaning – limit the physical involvement.

When a guy is comfortable, and he's basically getting from a girlfriend everything he would get from a wife, you will never really know if he's marriage-minded. Even he might not know. Remember the airplane that's circling the airport, but never lands? Because if there's no incentive for him, why should he upset the situation with commitment and marriage?

So don't be a wife to a boyfriend. We need to hold something back and get that plane to land. And then, if he's interested in marriage, and he likes you, he will get your contact info, he will call you, he will ask you out, he will keep asking you out, and he will keep pursuing you. You will not need to convert him, and you will not need to wonder if he's interested. It will be abundantly obvious.

Having Unrealistic Expectations

Here is a BIG one. A LOT of women trip up because they have unrealistic expectations about the dating process and what the guy they marry is going to be like. Let's look at a few of the unrealistic expectations we might have, so we can be sure not to make these mistakes.

Expecting Fireworks

One mistake is to expect that with the right guy, things will *click right away*. You'll just know, immediately, that he's the one. And you'll feel all these crazy feelings, like *I can't eat –* o*h, my gosh, I can't breathe!*

Occasionally you hear of a friend who knew right away. That's a huge blessing. But just because you heard of it happening here or there does not mean it's going to happen that way for you. The crazy fireworks feelings often go with infatuation, but not necessarily with love. You should feel *excited* when you decide to get married, but not necessarily so much intense drama. And realistically, it could take a few weeks or months before you feel like he really is the guy for you.

Expecting All the Good Traits

Sometimes, when people have been dating for a while, they kind of add together all the things they liked about all the people they ever dated and start looking for that. Okay, newsflash – this guy doesn't walk Planet Earth. This is why the deal-breaker list is so useful – it forces you to see what you're willing to compromise on and what you're not. You're not going to get some superhuman guy who is good-looking AND smart AND funny AND makes a ton of money AND is super kind, super driven, super chill AND has a great family AND is a cute Israeli AND is a fit, blond surfer, AND is super masculine and super sensitive, and so on and so on. These are the qualities of multiple different people! Instead, you need to always keep your personal deal-breakers front and center. Everything else is a bonus.

Expecting a Particular Physical Package

So many people get set on a specific *look*, or they fixate on some other superficial quality. Like, he has to be tall, or he has to be dark, or he has to be a lawyer or a doctor or whatever. I can't tell you how many times people end up marrying exactly the opposite of what they expect superficially.

Instead, be open, and don't get fixated on superficiality. When we let go of the physical expectations, we're learning a little humility in the face of the divine plan. Maybe I don't know exactly what would be right for me? Maybe God knows better than me? So be open-minded. And anything that can be easily changed, ignore for now. We can deal with it if it's really important to you. Remember – it's easier to build muscles than *middos*!

Expecting the Right Guy to Have No Flaws

Sometimes we expect our husband-to-be to have no flaws. But let's be honest – like we said in the beginning, Mr. Perfect doesn't exist. Everyone has flaws. Just like we do! So what's the real question you want to be asking yourself? Can I see his flaws? (If you can't, he's hiding something or you haven't been dating long enough.) And are his flaws things I can live with? Can I tolerate them? If they're not on your deal-breaker list, you probably want to accept that you can live with them. Because if we're breaking up with guys because they have flaws that aren't even that important to us, we may be losing out on the right guy. In other words, I can't be looking for someone that doesn't have *any* flaws. Or else, I'll always be looking.

Not Knowing Which Feelings to Take Seriously

Now we're going to shift a little bit. We've been talking about what we expect in the other person – but it's also important to understand how to relate to our own feelings during the dating process.

Don't Walk Away Just Because You're Anxious

Feeling anxious is not unusual during the dating process. And because of that anxiety, we might be inclined to break up with a particular person, even though he might be a great guy.

It's important to distinguish between our own baggage versus a valid concern in the relationship. And this is the kind of thing that we can't really figure out without outside help. It could be a therapist, it could be a mentor, or it could be a dating coach.

Marriage is a big decision, and we want to get it right. Of course it's stressful, and it's totally normal to be anxious. If you ever struggled with anxiety – like when you applied to college, or while working a stressful job – it's for sure going to be the same when you're dating. You're the same person, right? Whatever you look like when you're stressed could be how you will be when you're dating.

So don't take it as necessarily a deal-breaker if you have anxiety. Instead, look into what's causing your anxiety. Peel it apart and try to see – is this just my own stuff? Or is this really something significant in him or in our relationship that warrants my concern?

Batya's Story

A religious client of mine, Batya, was dating a guy for a month and a half. She was in her late twenties, which in the religious world is on the higher end. And her family was telling her, *if you don't know by now, then he's not your husband.*

Thank God, her married sister said, "You know what, before you break it off, just run it by Mrs. Kigel. I know she's a professional dating coach – run it by her just in case."

We sat down and went through the whole process. He matched her deal-breaker list completely, they had great conversations, mutual respect, she thought he was cute. Everything was there. It was just that the emotional connection and physical attraction was not where it needed to be.

Now, for women, as I've said, physical attraction often comes largely from emotional connection. And she was feeling neither of these to the level that getting engaged demands. I said to her, "You can't break off this relationship. Everything's there on paper, and he seems smitten" – which I pay attention to, since the guy often knows before the girl. "Instead, let's tweak the dating process a little bit. First, I want to take all the stress off you. You're not allowed to make a decision about the relationship for at least the next month."

She was giving herself so much stress, and her parents were stressing her out. *Everyone* was stressing her out. She didn't want to make the wrong decision (not surprisingly!), and it was driving her crazy!

In my professional experience, the same "radio frequency" that makes a woman feel anxious is the one that's involved in physical attraction. If you are consumed with anxiety, it's literally impossible to feel whether you are attracted to someone or not. All your headspace is consumed by the anxiety. I've had countless clients in this scenario.

I said to her, "We're taking the decision off the table. Your job is just to date him and enjoy yourself. Period, full stop. When you start analyzing whether he's your husband, visualize a big red stop sign!"

Then, on top of that, we tweaked things so they would go out more often. Twice a week for some people is not enough to develop a real connection. You need to have the person become part of your life. So, I had them go out three times a week. At the same time, I asked her if there were any moments during the dating process when she had felt more attracted and more drawn to him.

For her, it was when they were doing something fun. I had them do more fun stuff on dates – you know, mini golf, bowling, hiking, ice-skating, whatever. Whatever's working, do more of it!

This is what we do when everything looks good on paper, but you're just not feeling connected. Get rid of the anxiety and enjoy yourself with him and do more of the stuff that makes you feel attracted.

Less than a month later, she told me, "I'm so attracted to him!"

And yes, they're married.

Don't Ignore Your Gut

Sometimes, we may need to set our anxiety aside because it's not related to real issues in the relationship.

Other times, we really want to be paying attention to what our feelings are telling us – especially when they are deep in our gut. Sometimes your body picks up on information before your brain. So even if you're not sure why, but you are feeling in your gut unsafe or uncomfortable with someone, please pay attention to that. It's always good to run it by a mentor, obviously. You might be mistaken, right? But don't discount it. I will often speak to a client at length, teasing out when and why she is feeling anxious, to determine whether it's something significant or not.

By the same token, if you're already at the point where you've gotten engaged to someone, and you are significantly anxious, don't set a date for the wedding until you've resolved it by speaking to a coach or therapist. Sometimes this is a gut feeling that you really need to pay attention to.

I once had a woman, Andrea, come to me for *kallah* classes, which prepare a woman for her intimate life and marriage. And hearing her talk a little bit about the relationship, I put on my dating coach hat. I said, "This does not sound good to me. I'm

Handy Hebrew Helper: *Kallah* means "bride," and *kallah* classes are lessons in the laws of Jewish marriage that a Jewishly observant young woman takes before getting married to prepare her for her intimate life and marriage. Observant Jewish grooms also take classes to prepare them to be husbands.

begging you, push off the wedding and go to therapy together with him."

In the end, she felt very pressured by her family and her age, and she went through with the wedding. They got married and were divorced within six months. Thank God, she is happily married to someone else with a couple kids now.

Generally speaking, if everything was hunky-dory the whole dating period, and then all of a sudden, when you're talking about engagement, you start freaking out, that's usually a sign of garden-variety cold feet. It's probably not a big deal. But always check it out with a mentor.

But if there's been something nagging at you the whole time, and you kept pushing through and pushing through, and now you are really having serious anxiety or doubts during engagement, speak to someone. Don't just push through. Remember the advice the rabbi gave me before I broke off my engagement? It is so much easier to break an engagement than to get a divorce!

Don't Date Dysfunction Just Because It Feels Familiar

Sometimes a certain habit or behavior in a guy may feel familiar because we were exposed to it elsewhere in our lives – either in our family or in a significant relationship. And then it sort of feels right, even though it's really not healthy.

Keep your eyes open for this kind of dysfunction. This is where having a mentor is really important, so you can ask, "Is it normal that he said this? Or did that?" Someone told me recently that as their relationship went on, the guy would start saying,

"Where were you last night? Why couldn't I get in touch with you? Where were you at ten? Where were you at eleven?" This can definitely be a sign of controlling behavior.

You want to know the signs of a seriously unhealthy person, or at least have someone you can talk things through with in case you're not sure.

For instance, these are some signs of an unhealthy relationship:[2]

1. Showering you with affection early in the relationship. This is called "love bombing," and it can be a way for a person to try to get control over you early in the relationship.

2. Talking about an ex with disrespect. A person who constantly blames or badmouths an ex may very well be a person who has difficulty taking responsibility himself. Watch out!

3. Getting angry in a way that makes you feel unsafe. If your partner is getting angry and threatening to hurt you, or you feel otherwise unsafe around his anger – pay attention. Do not sweep this under the carpet. Everyone gets angry sometimes, but in a healthy relationship, we are not taking out our anger on one another.

4. Pushing your physical boundaries or disrespecting your personal space. This is when your partner is making you do things you're not comfortable with. If he's not listening to what you want, and he's regularly crossing personal lines, that's a sign of disrespect. Pay attention.

5. Isolating you. If he is trying to cut off your relationships to the outside world, including asking you to delete

---

2   Based on Cleveland Clinic, "How to Spot Relationship Red Flags," April 6, 2022, https://health.clevelandclinic.org/domestic-abuse-how-to -spot-relationship-red-flags/.

social media accounts, consider getting out right away. Isolating another person is a way to gain power in a relationship. The smaller they can make your world, the more they can control it.

6. They bombard you with constant messages and expect an immediate response. This is often another sign of someone looking to control a relationship. Talk to him early about your expectations around texting and other communication.

7. Making private concerns public. If he is posting on social media about issues in your relationship in a way that embarrasses or belittles you, don't lie down and take it. This is a sign of an unhealthy relationship, and you owe it to yourself to move on.

If you grew up around dysfunction, some of this stuff might feel comfortable or normal to you, even if you've worked really hard to get over it. Check it out with a third party, and don't just sweep it under the rug.

Being the Pursuer as a Woman

As we move into our last few dating don'ts, I want to talk about a few ways that we, as women, can inadvertently push the right guy away.

One common issue I see is the woman being the pursuer. As in, asking him out first, calling him, messaging him, texting him. You know, trying to move things along by prodding: "When are you free next?" or, "I'm free on Thursday."

Stop. Break your addiction. All dating books (Jewish and non-Jewish) say the same thing. As liberated and advanced as our society is, the average man wants to be the one pursuing and taking the active role.

If I'm doing all the work for him (texting first, asking him out, planning the dates, splitting the bill), how do I know if he's really interested in me? How will I ever know if he's valuing me and cares for me? Maybe it's just easy and comfortable for him?

If this is you, stop. Let him lead. No matter what your political perspective is. Trust me on this one. You don't want to be second-guessing whether he's really interested.

If you're not leading, and you want to know if he's interested – well, he asked you out. And he asked you out again. And he messaged you first. And he called you. Guess what? He's interested. As reality therapy founder Robert Wubbolding says, "Behavior is a language."[3] So just notice what your date is telling you through his actions.

We're tempted to reach out, especially when the guy is being lackadaisical about messaging us. *He let a bunch of days go by, maybe a week, so I think maybe he's ghosting me.*

Stop. Do not reach out. Sit on your hands. Go work out or call a friend instead. So stop chasing, and start attracting. You can communicate interest with a smile, a warm vibe, and a receptive energy.

Obviously, once you're serious and he's proved his interest level, you can reach out to him. Like, *I've always wanted to try this new sushi place in midtown – wanna make reservations?* But in the early stages of dating, do anything to distract yourself from waiting by the phone with your fingers itching to text him.

Being Good Friends with Other Men

Important piece of advice here. When you're looking for your husband, don't be *close* friends with other guys. Try to wean yourself off these relationships.

The reason is that you get very comfortable when you have close guy friends. You might not think about it this way, but we

---

3   Robert E. Wubbolding, John Brickell, "Purpose of Behavior: Language and Levels of Commitment," *International Journal of Reality Therapy* 25, no. 1 (Fall 2005): 41.

can actually satisfy a lot of our emotional relationship needs from a friendship with a guy. Instead, hang out with your girlfriends, go out with your sister, work out at the gym, stay busy.

When we have super close guy friends, it's almost like spiritually, there is someone blocking the door for Mr. Right to walk through. Because you've already filled that space with someone else.

Whereas if you want to find the guy you want to *marry* and not just the guy you want to be friends with, you have to keep that special spot unoccupied so it's ready for him to fill it.

Basically, we need to KonMari our dating life – clear out all the clutter and deadwood. This includes exes you're still in touch with (why are you still texting him?!) and also close guy friends. You have loose strings of emotions for these people. You're entangled with them. Instead, close the door, wish them well, and go forward with a clear heart and mind.

Something-Better-around-the-Corner Syndrome

This can be particularly dicey for those of us in the New York area, where the quantity of eligible Jewish singles is like…through the roof. So it's very common to think, "Yeah, he's good. But what if I were to find all of that, but also, he was really wealthy?"

Ladies, let's not catch the something-better-around-the-corner syndrome. There's always going to be a guy who is better looking, wealthier, or more ambitious, smarter, or whatever.

Keep the question clear and simple: Is the person I'm dating *right now*, with his unique combination of qualities and strengths, the right one for me? Don't forget your deal-breaker list – it's your best tool for figuring this out.

It's important to stay in the present. Don't ask, "What about that guy I was messaging yesterday? Maybe he's better?" Instead, clear your head and just focus on the guy in front of you. Is he a mensch? Do I trust him? Do I respect him? Does he have the core things I'm looking for? Do we have common goals and values?

How's the attraction? If everything checks out, we literally close our eyes to all the other guys and don't look back.

Dating More Than One Person at a Time

This kind of goes without saying, but generally speaking, we want to date one person at a time. Dating multiple people tends to make us very confused. First of all, you forget what story you told to whom. And you start to go back to something he said and then realize, *Oh, no, that was the other guy!* Awkward.

But it also gets confusing in terms of getting clarity on the relationship. It's just very hard to give one guy serious consideration when you're seeing another in the same time frame. So in general, we try to date one person at a time. We want to avoid "choice paralysis" – having too many choices and so making none.[4]

Now, sometimes it doesn't work out that way in the beginning. Perhaps someone suggested someone to you. But by the time he called you, you had already met someone else at an event and went on a first date. So am I going to say that dating more than one person at a time should *never* happen? No, it's not a hard-and-fast rule.

But if it does happen that you end up dating more than one person at once, the goal should be to get clarity *as soon as possible* so you can say no to whoever you're not interested in. And then focus only on the guy with serious potential. The stage where you're dating more than one person should not last very long. And for the girls who are dating in the *shidduch* world (the Orthodox system), we date one at a time for sure.

By the way, it's easier to rule someone out than rule someone in – meaning that just because we decided to go with choice

---

4   Barry Schwartz, *The Paradox of Choice: Why More Is Less; How the Culture of Abundance Robs Us of Satisfaction* (New York: Harper Perennial, 2005). See also his TED Talk "The Paradox of Choice," https://www.ted.com/talks/barry_schwartz_the_paradox_of_choice.

number 2 doesn't mean he's our husband; it just means he's more of a contender. I have to reassure many of my clients: if you say yes to the next date, it doesn't mean you have to marry him!

Schlepping Out the Dating Process

For our final don't, we have to talk about schlepping out the dating process. Basically, life is short. We want to spend our time with our future husband, not with all the guys we need to date before we're able to meet him. We want to date efficiently and not waste time!

To do this, we need to make sure all our dates have a purpose. We are learning something new about him each time. We're not watching movies, going to loud concerts, going on group dates, or fooling around. We're introducing topics that will help us get to know each other in a deep way. We're seeing if we are bonding emotionally with this person.

Use a dating game if you want to get ideas of what to talk about to move things along. If you're getting stuck on "what should we talk about next?" it's an easier way to get into deeper conversations.

A few examples of things you can talk about might be:

- What made you decide to choose this line of work or go to this school?
- If he's becoming more connected to Judaism: What spurred you on your spiritual journey?
- Did you ever go to Israel? What did you do there?
- How did you grow up? Did your mom work? Did she not work? How do you feel about how you grew up?
- How did you grow up financially?
- Did your family take vacations?
- Do you want children? How many?
- How do you envision raising children?
- What communities do you like spending time in?

As the dates pass and you keep getting more information, you should be going back to your deal-breaker list to see if he matches up with it. If he does, and you're feeling the attraction go up, great! Keep it up. If things have flatlined (and tweaking things hasn't worked) or he's missing some of your must-haves from your deal-breaker list, it's time to end it – even if you have great chemistry or you like a lot of things about him. Don't waste your time or his. Tell yourself, *My husband is waiting for me! I can't waste my time!* And then move on.

Chapter 8

How Hollywood Love Confuses Us

Have you ever watched a romantic comedy? Maybe it was a Disney movie or a Tom Hanks movie or a soap opera? And it wasn't just *a* movie, or *a* show, right? But movie after movie (sometimes even the same movie over and over again... *When Harry Met Sally*, anyone?) and show after show since we were young, and all through adulthood.

Of course, we all know intellectually that these movies and shows aren't *real*. But when we see the same values promoted in storylines, continuously over a long period of time, the line between fantasy and reality tends to get blurred. And we start to think that real life is how it looks in the movies.

The Disney Version of Love

When I interview a client for the first time, I will usually be able to tell how much media she's been exposed to by the way she describes what she's looking for.

If the word *cool* is used, that means she's watched a lot of movies and TV. Because *cool* is not a Jewish vocabulary word. What does it even mean? He dresses well? He does his hair? Basically, he's trying to sweet-talk you. It's a curated vibe that really doesn't have much to do with inner character or marriage material.

When we're exposed to this stuff over and over from such a young age, there is no question that we are subconsciously influenced.

And then, based on this super magical, fantastical idea of love that we start to pick up, how often do two people stop working on their marriage, God forbid, and instead look elsewhere? Just to recreate the excitement, the passion of new love that they got hooked on by watching all these movies and soap operas?

One of my favorite examples of getting problematic messages from movies is *Sleepless in Seattle* (such a fun movie, but…). It's about a man and a woman who learn about each other and are kind of interested in each other, but have never met. And it's like…*will they meet, will they meet?* And when they finally do, that's the end of the movie.

They haven't even had a conversation. But they're just *destined* to be together. We have no idea if they have common goals and values. We don't know if they meet each other's fundamental needs. Who knows? Who cares? And then in the last three seconds of the movie, they finally meet and we're assuming sail happily ever after into the sunset. So what is this movie telling us about love? And about the process of deciding if someone is *the one*? I always wanted to see a sequel – once the infatuation wore off and they had to work on their relationship!

Another one of my favorite movies of all time is the movie *Enchanted*. The prince reaches up to catch her, and she falls from the tree into his arms. And of course, they've never met before. They've never even said two words to each other. And he says, "We'll be married in the morning!"

In this movie, Disney is making fun of itself. But what's not a joke is that this is literally the message Disney has been sending for years and years in so many of its movies. And we've all watched so many of them that they start to penetrate deep into our subconscious minds: *You don't really have to have conversations! You're just destined to be together. The chemistry is there. There's a "click" immediately. It's fireworks! Let's get married!*

Soap operas also provide a very unrealistic view of marriage and love. And on top of that, the plotlines always involve infidelity. So you have a classic couple, like Bo and Hope on *Days of Our Lives*, and they've been married for like…three hundred years. But then, to spice things up and make people watch the show, they both have romantic dalliances with other people. This is such an awful message.

I want to identify a little more clearly what the messages are that we get from movies and the media. And then we will switch gears and examine the Jewish approach to love and relationships and how they compare.

True Love Is "Falling"

The first message we get from secular media is that loving a person is *falling for them*. Meaning, it *just happens* – sometimes against your will and better judgment. Now, the person you stumbled for could be abusive, he could be a jerk, he could be missing your entire deal-breaker list. But you don't care, because you *fell*. And there's nothing to do when you fall, right? Because it's not a conscious decision.

In Judaism, we believe that we're *stepping* consciously into a relationship. It's not out of my control. I might have certain feelings without planning to have them, but what I do about my feelings is in my control.

I work with my clients to understand that we don't just fall for someone we have physical chemistry with. We want to make a conscious choice to build a relationship with a mensch who has what we are looking for long-term. We want to focus more on his actions, not simply his words. We want to date in reality as opposed to living in a fantasy we're making up in our head.

We're Not Responsible for What We Do

The whole concept behind all the infidelity in the soap operas is that "I can't help myself." It just happens. My body took control. Similar to falling: *it just happened.*

So many people ask me why I became religious. Honestly, it was not for some holy or spiritual reason in the beginning. Really, it was because I was sick of the "boys will be boys" mentality in the secular world. I was disgusted by the idea that a married man would say, "My secretary looked good; I couldn't help it."

And then I learned from a Jewish perspective that we all contain a piece of God inside us and that we're not just a body, not just an intelligent baboon. We are a soul that helps the body to make moral choices.

True freedom is the ability to refrain from what your body naturally wants to do. Otherwise, you're just a slave to your inner baboon. That is what appealed to me when I first learned about the concept of *shomer negiyah*, not touching during dating. Because it was about self-mastery.

It says in *Pirkei Avot*, Ethics of Our Fathers, "Who is a strong man? He who conquers his [evil] inclination."[1] In other words, the man who can control himself, who has self-mastery, is the true hero.

Love and Lust Are Synonymous

If you think about it, in the media, there's not that much difference between love and lust. If he *wants* her, if he's *attracted* to her – that means he also must *love* her. Which means that love is completely chemically based. It's the same thing as infatuation – that *drive-me-crazy, can't-stop-thinking-about-you* feeling that so many movies and shows are about.

With infatuation, your brain is completely checked out. You have zero rational thought going on. You're being controlled by your hormones and chemistry.

Now, I know this might be *exciting*. And yeah, it might feel good short-term to be infatuated. But is this the same thing as love?

We'll talk about the Jewish perspective on love in a little bit. Suffice it to say, in Judaism, love and lust are definitely *not* the same thing.

---

1   *Pirkei Avot* 4:1.

We're All Wrong, but Yet So Right

When we believe that lust and love are the same thing, what does that lead to? Imagine a couple who are totally mismatched, but the chemistry is so strong, they're just going to go for it anyway. This is a perfect picture of what happens when you believe that love and infatuation are the same thing: you end up with a guy you have great chemistry with, but who is *so* wrong for you!

And this is totally the opposite of what I teach my clients, which is obviously sticking to your deal-breaker list like it's the Ten Commandments, *no matter how strong the chemistry might be.* It's also critical to look for those key ingredients: Is there mutual respect? Does he have good character? Is he growth-oriented? We're not going for *we're all wrong and he treats me terribly, but I just can't help myself.* That is complete insanity!

The Bad Boy Will Change for the Right Girl

"I love projects," or, "Meeting me will make him want to get married," said many women throughout history while they were making the biggest mistake of their lives.

I know you've seen it in the movies. I know it is *so* romantic when the bad boy falls for the sweet, beautiful girl and totally changes his ways. But in real life, this does not happen.

You are not going to reform the bad boy. If he's a player when he meets you, chances are that he will continue to be a player for a long time after he's met you. You are not going to change that – so stop trying! Let's find a mensch who is already marriage-minded and is not going to break your heart into a million pieces before you figure out that he still is not going to change.

Looks and Image Create Long-Term Happiness

If there's anything that Hollywood has injected into our brains over and over again, it's that looks, image, wealth, and status create long-term happiness. When all you see are these super fit, super attractive guys on screen, falling in love with beautiful girls, it is easy to start to believe that looks, wealth, and status are really important for long-term happiness in a marriage.

And I do have some clients who will say to me, "He needs to be six feet and gorgeous and wealthy." Does any of this contribute to a solid, eternal marriage? Most people gain weight, every guy eventually loses his hair, and money comes and goes.

If you are going to marry someone based on superficial, conditional things like that, you're setting yourself up for a terrible marriage and perhaps even divorce. We don't want to be marrying someone for something conditional and external like beauty, money, or image. We want to be focused primarily on the inner core – his character and whether he matches your deal-breaker list.

One of my mentors, Rebbetzin Esther Jungreis, wrote in her book *The Committed Life* about how easily young women are impressed by a handsome or apparently successful young man: "Do they know anything about him? Do they know whether he is kind or self-centered, wise or foolish, or do they consider what sort of father he will one day be to their children?"[2] As she points out, a man can always improve his financial standing, educational status, or wardrobe, but if he isn't a good man, why would you want to marry him in the first place?

Physical Intimacy Leads to Marriage

In pretty much every modern movie and soap opera, the physical comes very quickly and the happily ever after inevitably follows. This makes sense if love is based mostly on physical attraction and chemistry, right? If everything goes well with the test drive, you might as well get married.

---

2   Rebbetzin Esther Jungreis, *The Committed Life: Principles for Good Living from Our Timeless Past* (New York: Cliff Street Books/HarperCollins, 1998), 262.

But in real life, having physical intimacy lead to marriage is…not so common. A lot of times when things get physical, they stay physical and never get any deeper…and then the relationship eventually blows up into tiny pieces when the couple start fighting and disrespecting each other because they never had anything in common anyway. And good character? Yeah, not a priority.

As I've already said, I teach women to date smart, which means shelving the physical, at least for the beginning of the relationship. If you let the chemistry take over, it can be really hard to be objective about whether this is really a person you want to spend your life with.

In the Jewish world, we literally do the opposite of Hollywood. We totally flip it around. First we determine if the person is compatible with us, and then we invest a little bit more emotionally, and only after we're deeply connected emotionally and he matches our deal-breaker list and we've made a commitment to this person (marriage) do we start a physical relationship.

Rebbetzin Jungreis wrote with piercing honesty about what can happen when a young woman does not keep this boundary and gives a man the benefits of marriage without any of the responsibilities: "That's the big mistake all of you girls make…. You move in with him, so now he has a girlfriend, a cook, a housekeeper, a companion – all free of charge with no responsibilities. You convince yourself that you can trust him when he says, 'Eventually we'll get married, honey. I'm just not ready yet.' A year goes by, then two…with every year that passes, the prospect of having a family becomes more remote…" And before you know it, it's another break-up and more time that was stolen from you.[3]

You'll Know Instantly When You Meet the One

The myth that love is instant can be so destructive to people who are looking to get married. People get fixated on the erroneous

---

3   Jungreis, *The Committed Life*, 263.

idea that you'll know when you've met *the one* right away. It's the click, the electricity, the chemistry. Seeing him across the room and locking eyes. *Crackle, crackle.* There's electricity in the room! It must be the right person! And I know right away because the feeling of meeting him is so intense, it will be totally obvious.

Now, it's true, this happens occasionally, and it's a big gift. But frankly, it's very rare.

The reality is that guy you locked eyes with and felt destined to be with…could be totally the wrong person. The vast majority of my clients thought their husband-to-be was a little cute when they first met. Not necessarily anything amazing. But then, as they got to know him better, the more they saw good qualities in him and the more attracted they became. That's usually a healthy, normal progression in a relationship for a woman.

So, no fireworks, no magic in the air instantaneously. No love at first sight. You might feel magical a few months in. But we are not giving up on a relationship because we don't feel it right away.

We want to lead with our head and bring our heart and hormones along *after*. It's not that our heart and hormones don't count. By the time we take our leap of faith, we want them on the bandwagon too! But they should definitely not be leading the process.

Love Lasts Forever If You Choose Properly

The other thing we get from movies is that love lasts forever, as long as you choose properly. Hollywood tells us all you have to do is find the right guy and then you can sail off into the sunset blissfully… But as those of us who are married will attest, it's a lot of work to stay married, even if you chose the right person for you.

Each member of a married couple is a different person; they each have different families, different backgrounds, sometimes different cultures. And if you're older when you get married, it's much harder to mesh with another person, because you've been doing everything your way for thirty or forty years. I've heard it described as a "merger" marriage versus a "start-up" marriage (another reason marriages in the Orthodox world are by and large more successful, because people in this community generally get married younger and are able to build a life together).

The adjustment is really hard. Why are we surprised when it's hard? Maybe because we've been brainwashed to think that as long as we chose properly, marriage should just flow. Very few movies show you the real work of marriage.

My favorite line about marriage is that when you're dating, you need to keep both eyes wide open (to catch red flags and incompatibilities)…but once you're under the chuppah, you close one eye (to the negatives that you agreed to have forbearance about).

So the Jewish message is happily ever after…with a lot of work!

*   *   *

Can you see how these messages about love and marriage might mess with your dating process? It's no wonder the secular dating world is so upside down and backwards!

Chapter 9

The Jewish View of Love

N ow that we've used our brains to look at the messages we get from movies and soap operas about love, and we've realized just how crazy and dangerous these ideas can be, let's take a look at the Jewish view of love, which gives us the Jewish way of dating and the path to a long, happy, successful marriage. What is the Jewish approach? Is there a different way to think about this?

I know you know the answer. But I'll say it anyway. Yes!

Love Is Giving

We already saw that secular culture seems to be really confused about the difference between love and lust. So many of the other mistaken messages stem from this confusion, if you think about it. If love and lust are the same, I might think that I should start with the physical and then see if a relationship builds from there. I might think that I should marry the guy who's so wrong for me because we're so right chemically. I might think that love is something totally out of my control…because my body basically just falls into it. So getting this straight is really important.

Now we're ready to hear what Judaism has to say.

Rabbi Aryeh Kaplan says that love and lust should not be confused.[1] Lust wants to *take*. It's all about what you want. It's really just an expression of physical desire, the same as being

---

1   Rabbi Aryeh Kaplan, *Made in Heaven: A Jewish Wedding Guide* (New York: Moznaim, 1983).

113

hungry or being tired. It's the body saying, "I'm hungry for physical contact right now. And I want it from you."

Love, on the other hand, wants to *give*. It's about each person seeing the other person and giving to one another. And the Torah's paradigm of love is to "love your neighbor as yourself." The goal is to be so concerned with or interested in the other person that we feel the same way about the other person as we feel about ourselves.

This is a feeling that usually develops over time, so don't be alarmed if you don't feel this right away with the man you are dating (especially if you have a brief courtship through the *shidduch* system). But just know that eventually, loving your spouse means not "falling for" him but giving to him on a level equal to the way you want to give to or take care of yourself.

This is much easier to feel with children. If you're a mom and your kid gets injured, you would a million times over stick yourself in the operating room instead of your kid if you could. It is so much more painful when your child is suffering than when you're suffering. But that is really ideally how we're supposed to feel about our spouse as well.

When you truly love someone, that person's happiness is as important to you as your own happiness. You're as happy for their successes as for your own, and you don't view it as a competition. That's real love.

Gila Manolson speaks about this in her book *Head to Heart*.[2] People often approach love as a sensation based on physical and emotional attraction that spontaneously generates when Mr. or Mrs. Right is around. But the issue with this is that it can just as easily spontaneously *degenerate* when the magic isn't there anymore. If you can fall *in love*, you can fall *out of love*, right? And we

---

2   Gila Manolson, *Head to Heart: What to Know before Dating and Marriage* (Nanuet, NY: Feldheim, 2002).

all know there are people who sadly get divorced, who say they just "fell out of love."

But of course, as we said, that is not a Jewish concept. The Hebrew word *ahavah*, which means "love," comes from the word *hav*, which means "give." For instance, you love your newborn baby even though the baby has done nothing for you and spits up on you and screams his or her head off. Why? Because you've been giving to your baby twenty-four seven since before the baby was born.

> **Handy Hebrew Helper:** *Ahavah* means "love." It comes from the root word *hav*, which means "give." For our purposes, this is a reminder that you love what you give to.

This is why when we want to increase the love in our marriage, instead of going all Janet Jackson and asking, "What have you done for me lately?" let's ask, "What have I done *for you* lately?" And the thing is, it's contagious. He'll probably start giving more to you in response.

Does Chemistry Still Play a Role?

You might be wondering, if love is about giving, why do we sometimes have such strong feelings of infatuation or chemistry? Are these meant to play a role in our relationship at all?

The answer is yes. We're not *ignoring* chemistry altogether. We just don't want it to be the main focus.

Chana Levitan speaks about the trap of infatuation.[3] She writes that the relationship between love and infatuation (for our purposes, I prefer to say "chemistry") is like making a campfire. To build a fire, you need large logs, but you also need twigs, paper, and matches as your starters. Try kindling logs directly, and you'll be waiting all night. But if you don't have any logs,

---

3   Chana Levitan, *I Only Want to Get Married Once: Dating Secrets for Getting It Right the First Time* (Jerusalem: Gefen Publishing House, 2010).

and you just light the twigs and paper, the fire will burn bright for a very short time, and then it will go out. So you need both kindling and fuel.

Chemistry is the twigs and the paper. It can play an important role in igniting the logs of love. But you must make sure infatuation isn't the foundation of your relationship. When you get carried away with the chemistry and forget about the substance of the relationship, chances are you'll end up brokenhearted. It's just a matter of time before the fire fizzles and burns out.

The Oneness of Man and Woman

Now, intuitively, we know that love is about giving. And the more we give to someone, the more we will love that person. Like we love our kids because we give nonstop to them. But it's still kind of a question – why do we need to be in marriage relationships at all? Obviously, people technically need to get together to have children. But is there anything more to it?

Obviously, in the Jewish perspective, the answer is going to be yes. The twentieth-century English rabbi Eliyahu Dessler says that the source of the love between a man and woman is the fact that they complete each other.[4] Meaning, in His great and ultimate wisdom, God created men and women to be *incomplete on their own*. By ourselves, we are literally not whole. This is why God, in the Garden of Eden, said, "It is not good that the man should be alone; I will make him a helpmate for him" (Genesis 2:18).

Then, when we get together as part of a marriage, and we work on our relationship and create harmony in our family by giving what the other person needs, we become whole. And since we really want to be whole, a part of us is always looking for that relationship until we've found it.

4   *Strive for Truth! Michtav Me'Eliyahu: Selected Writings of Rabbi Eliyahu Eliezer Dessler* (Spring Valley, NY: Feldheim, 1988), 131.

Does this mean we're supposed to totally negate ourselves and dissolve into a marriage? No. Even though we are achieving a kind of unity, true love shouldn't get rid of our individuality. Instead, it's meant to teach us not to be selfish.

We come into this world as a little baby whose attitude is "Me, me, me, gimme, gimme, gimme, now, now, now, scream, scream, scream." And our goal over the course of our lifetime is to become a person who is a giver, who thinks about other people and not just about ourselves.

Marriage can create an amazing unity where one plus one equals one. And we get there by learning to be better givers. Believe me, marriage is the best laboratory to work on becoming a giver, because marriage, and especially parenthood, means you're not living on your own time. You're there to give – whatever they need, when they need it. It really causes you to stretch yourself.

One of the words in Hebrew for marriage is *nisuin*, which actually means "to carry a burden." And that's really what marriage is according to Judaism – it's carrying the other person's burden, lightening their load. Though there may be times when you need to address things that you want your spouse to help you more with, you also want to be thinking, what am I doing? What's my part in this, and am I carrying his burden?

When we do this successfully, we achieve really great things. Rabbi Aryeh Kaplan states that neither male nor female alone was created in the image of God.[5] Rather, male and female *together* were created in the image of God. This means that when a man and a woman are together in perfect harmony, that's when they're really tapping into the image of God. And of course, when that happens, the potential to create life is also there. That's the power that makes us most similar to God – this ability to create life.

---

5   Rabbi Aryeh Kaplan, *Made in Heaven: A Jewish Wedding Guide* (New York: Moznaim, 1983), 12–13.

Rav Noach Weinberg defined love as identifying the other person with his virtues, rather than his faults. Meaning, everyone has faults, but once we're married, we want to choose to focus as much as possible on the good rather than the bad. This will cause love to grow, rather than die over time.

When we start to understand all of this, it makes a little more sense why marriage is hard work and why giving is so important. If the purpose of life is to stretch us and help us refine our character, we can't come into the world with everything being all peaches and cream and complete. What would be the point then?

So God created a masterful design in which He split us off from our other half and made it so that we would always want to come back to oneness. But to make that oneness happen, we would have to give and give and give and stretch ourselves and grow in the process. And only through this process of getting back to being complete by improving our character do we emulate God.

When we can achieve that with a spouse, our love will continue, and our lives will be filled with happiness and satisfaction.

The Power of Shared Goals

All of the above ideas about oneness are kind of on the spiritual side. But on the practical side, where do we see our oneness playing out in the strongest way? Rabbi Aharon Feldman wrote that a marriage whose goal is the marriage itself becomes filled with a sense of emptiness and will wither and die.[6] In other words, marriage is not meant to be a permanent date. It can't just be about doing fun things together. Date night is very important – of course you have to still have fun in your marriage! But it can't be the whole picture.

---

6   Rabbi Aharon Feldman, *The River, The Kettle and the Bird: A Torah Guide to Successful Marriage* (Jerusalem: CSB Publications, 1987), 141.

Instead, a married couple must be moving toward *common goals* if love is to continue to develop between them. What might be some common goals? Having children. Saving for a house. Building a business. Starting a nonprofit. Hosting guests in their home. When a couple works together toward something, it deepens their ties.

But here's the thing: the more important the goals that you share together, the deeper the emotional bonds created by working towards achieving them. Which means that a marriage is successful in proportion to the meaningfulness of the couple's shared goals.

In the Jewish world, nothing is as meaningful as the goal of making one's home into a sanctuary for the Divine. A Jewish home built on the Torah, in which the couple is raising children growing up with Torah, is the most meaningful thing that you could devote yourself to.

I have a friend who said to me, "You know, Devorah, you're doing so much cool stuff, you're traveling, speaking, running a business. And I'm just like…a mom."

> **Handy Hebrew Helper:** *Bli ayin hara* literally means "without the evil eye," and it is an expression often inserted after delivering happy news in the hopes of staving off bad luck.

I said to her, "There's nothing more important that you could be doing than raising really healthy, happy children. And despite all the exciting things that I'm doing, there is nothing that I view on my resume as more of an accomplishment than having a great marriage and raising four healthy children, *bli ayin hara*."

So Judaism can be the focal point of a couple's shared goals and it can make their union very meaningful. But no matter what your shared goals are, we always want to view ourselves as a team. If we constantly focus on the fact that we're a team, and we're one, we can avoid 80 percent of issues in our marriage, because so many conflicts are about defending my ego. If I view myself as on the same side, as one with him, I'm going to have a whole different attitude. It's not easy. But it is well worth it.

A Committed Relationship

Maybe by now this is obvious, but we're going to say it anyway. Rabbi Menachem Schlanger writes that within marriage, the unique qualities of a woman can assist and benefit her husband, since they're directed toward one particular man.[7] Similarly, the man is able to truly give to his wife when he is dedicated to just one woman. In other words, you get the best results in marriage when each person is faithful to the other in a completely committed way. The very basis of any constructive relationship between spouses is the exclusivity of the relationship. You're for me, and I'm for you.

Lastly, when a couple knows that God is watching them, it helps to ensure fidelity, commitment, and hard work, rather than dumping the relationship like a quick return at Costco.

So now that we've looked at the messages we got from Hollywood and the messages we get from the Torah about love, do you feel there's a winner here?

I mean, it depends what you want. A long-lasting committed marriage with a mensch? Or…years and years of dating different people and having your heart broken into a gazillion pieces? If you want the heartbreak, by all means, stick with Hollywood! But if you're looking for the long-lasting loving marriage, maybe it's time to get these Hollywood messages out of our brains and start thinking a little more in line with our Jewish roots.

Jews have always made marriage and family a priority. Part of how we've succeeded for generations is bringing a uniquely Jewish

---

7 Rabbi Menachem Schlanger, *Al Ptacheinu* (Jerusalem: Menachem Schlanger, 2012), 33.

approach to dating. You've learned the Jewish way of dating. And now you've learned about the Jewish view of love.

It's time to jump into the game to find Mr. Perfect-for-You, and get ready to build the marriage you've been waiting for!

A Parting Message

The journey to find Mr. Perfect-for-You is not easy. It's fraught with confusion, rejection, frustration, and dashed hopes. However, by utilizing timeless Jewish wisdom to date smarter, you can make the process far easier, calmer, and more efficient. My job is a happy one – I get to see hundreds of women go from hopeless to hopeful to happy! It makes my week when a client gets engaged to the right person for her! I hope you will be in touch with me if you want more personalized guidance. May you find your Mr. Right soon!

Frequently Asked Questions

Q: How can you know if he is the type of person who will raise his voice?

A: If you wait long enough, something will happen that should show you whether he has a temper. Watch how he reacts! You could also ask someone who knows him how they would describe him, and then just *wait for them to answer*. The first few words should tell you a lot. Then ask if they've ever seen him angry. You can find out a lot this way!

Q: What is your view on age difference?

A: I don't really think there's an issue with age difference. I have friends who married guys four years younger and friends who married guys ten to fourteen years older. You're young as long as you keep changing and growing. So if you feel like you're with your grandfather – or your teenage brother – that's not a go. But if personality and vibe work, don't stress the age.

Q: When do you meet the family?

A: It really depends on the world that you're dating in. In the religious world, the girl's family meets the guy right away, and the girl meets his family once it gets serious. In the secular world, you're probably not going to meet his parents until a little bit farther along. Either way, it's definitely important to get to know his family, because it gives you a better sense of who he is.

Q: Should you end a relationship because of his family?
A: I wouldn't brush everything under the carpet. Don't say, *everyone's dysfunctional, but I'll handle it*. However, a guy's family is also not his fault. I wouldn't rule someone out simply because of his upbringing if he has everything you're looking for. So, it's really case by case. Check this out with a mentor.

Q: When should level of religious observance be brought up?
A: In the religious world, we find out these answers even before the first date. For the rest of us, this should be brought up early on in the process (around dates 2-4) so that you don't waste time with someone who's completely incompatible.

Q: When working with a matchmaker, can you bring up going from two to three dates per week?
A: Yes, you can! This is the beauty of using an intermediary when you date – they can bring these things up for you. If you're dating a guy and don't have a matchmaker, you can ask on the date, "How do you feel about putting someone in the middle?" Then it's much easier for the person in the middle to say, "You know, now is a good time to take it up to three times a week."

Q: Should I still be *shomer* if I'm dating for a second marriage?
A: Yes, totally! If this is your second time around, all the more reason to take the physical off the table so you can pick up on every red flag.

Q: What should I do if a guy gets annoyed when I don't text him back right away?
A: Too bad for him! It doesn't matter if he gets annoyed that you didn't respond right away. Your future husband should understand that sometimes, a girl is busy. And frankly, texting is not my favorite way for you to communicate. Too many opportunities

for misunderstandings, and you're not able to pick up on body language or facial expressions.

Q: How can I see if a guy has commitment issues in a *shomer* relationship?
A: That's really the beauty of this system. If he isn't serious, he's not gonna stick around! There might be the rare guy who has commitment issues here. But mostly, this way of dating is going to weed them out.

Q: When should I decide to end a relationship because of a lack of chemistry?
A: Assuming he matches your deal-breaker list and you're just waiting on attraction, there is no mathematical formula. I would say that I don't think you should end something until you're really sure that you've given it your all and it's a firm no. I have clients who are happily married, whose attraction did not really kick in until several weeks in.

Q: How do you differentiate between cold feet and a real issue in the relationship – like feeling unsafe?
A: If your anxiety is more about the decision because you don't want to make a mistake, I would say that's usually cold feet. If you feel unsafe, uncomfortable, that you can't be yourself, or that he's making you feel insecure, those could be red flags. Either way, check with a mentor!

Q: What if the guy is just plain boring?
A: Obviously, you can't marry someone who's totally boring to you. If you really have nothing to say to each other, it's probably not a match. But this could just be a case of Mr. Pareve. If you give it long enough and work a little harder – go out more often, have deeper conversations, play a dating game – he might move to Mr. Yay! Give him a chance and see if anything develops.

Q: How can you figure out if he's seeing multiple women?
A: There's no way to know for sure unless he (or someone else) tells you. But he should be making time twice a week to see you. If he's never available, one possibility is that he's juggling several people. (Another is that he's simply not marriage-minded.)

Q: How do you know if he's a good guy?
A: For one, you have to date long enough to see for yourself what vibe you get from him. Is he compassionate? Respectful? Cares about what's important to you? Asks about you? Don't expect him to be attentive every second of every day – we all make mistakes and are sometimes insensitive. But in general, you should get the vibe that he's a good guy. You can also ask around! What other people say can be very telling.

Q: If a guy is not actively pursuing you, does it mean he's just not good at talking to girls?
A: I honestly don't think so. I think no matter how quiet or reserved the guy is, if he's marriage-minded, and he likes you, he'll ask you out. He'll pursue you. Guys are guys, and when they meet the right person, they will move heaven and earth to marry her!

Q: When you've been disappointed many times, how do you recover?
A: Number one, take a break! It doesn't matter how old you are. You don't have to date constantly. It's not healthy. Give yourself time to recover. And during your break, nurture yourself, do tons of self-care, things that make you happy. And when you're ready to jump back in, focus on networking rather than going to singles events. Events can make you very burnt out. Also, if you keep being disappointed, it's possible that you're not being discerning enough – you don't have to say yes to everyone who's suggested to you. Being selective is not "picky."

Q: What if no one is coming close to matching my deal-breaker list?

A: I don't like to say this flippantly. But if you are getting to the point where you feel that no one makes it into the ball-park, it could be that your qualifications are too narrow. I never want you to settle, but at the same time, it's *very* important that our deal-breakers are only things we truly must have or really can't deal with, and we're not saying no to people who actually could be for us. Check with a mentor to see if your list is reasonable.

Q: How do you know if you're setting your standards too high?

A: This is really an individual thing. But a person should never get to the chuppah and think *he's getting a good deal marrying me!* You shouldn't feel that you're settling. You should be excited to marry him. Now, excitement looks different on every person at every age. But it really comes down to the deal-breaker list and whether you've made it correctly. Sometimes people put things that are really *wants* alongside *needs*. And that might mean your standards are not realistic.

Q: What if everything makes sense on paper but I don't feel excited?

A: So first of all, are you telling me that you went out two, three, four times with him and you don't feel anything? You didn't give it enough time. Keep going out. Mr. Pareve can become Mr. Yay! If you're telling me you dated him for a few months, and you're not feeling excited, then it might be a case of good on paper, but this is not my husband. This is rare, but it can happen. Either way, speak to a mentor before breaking it off. You can use different tricks to try to spark those feelings that you're missing. It's worth trying.

Q: What are your thoughts on dating or marriage across different cultural backgrounds?

A: I don't think it's a deal-breaker. (I married a Russian guy, remember?) But I will tell you that it can be challenging. It's certainly easier to marry someone whose background is similar to yours. So it's not something to be entered into lightly.

Q: How do you bring up how you want to raise your kids in a way that feels natural?

A: I think a very good way of doing this is talking about communities that you've spent time in. Have you ever spent time in Teaneck, or the Five Towns, or Monsey or Denver or LA? How did you like it? What did you like? What did you not like? You can also talk about how he grew up or where he went to school and what he liked about it and what he didn't. And don't forget to discuss whether you'd want to send your kids to yeshiva, day school, or public school.

Acknowledgments

This book, which has resided in my head for years, could not have materialized into reality without the help and guidance of many people. Ilan Greenfield at Gefen Publishing House, who believed in my book, and his chief editor, Kezia Raffel Pride, who smoothed out the rough edges and made it so much easier to read. Emunah Fialkoff, who helped get my notes, ideas, and classes into a more legible format. Moshe Gersht, who helped guide me to take my coaching to the next level and encouraged me to stay true to my values. My clients, students, and friends, who read drafts of the book and gave their feedback. Jodi Samuels and Steve Eisenberg, who gave me my first teaching gig at JICNY back in 2002 and saw a superpower in me that I did not know was there. Judith Rosenbluth and Lauren Levy, who help me with my social media and website, respectively. My parents, who raised me to think deeply and pursue truth. My in-laws, who raised a mensch! My husband, Reuven, who is my soulmate and biggest fan. My children – Dalia, Kayla, Yoni, and Moshe – who are the most significant accomplishments of my life and are always "coaching" their friends (future business partners?). My sons-in-law, two mensches who joined our family. And last but most important, my Creator, Who brought me on quite an interesting journey and gave me certain gifts, which I am hopefully using to make His world a little bit more loving.